.hack//

Another Birth

vol.1//INFECTION_

**Story by
Miyu Kawasaki**

**Supervised by
Kazunori Ito**

**Illustrated by
CyberConnect2 Ito**

TOKYOPOP®

HAMBURG // LONDON // LOS ANGELES // TOKYO

.hack//Another Birth
Story by Miu Kawasaki
Supervised by Kazunori Ito
Illustrated by CyberConnect2

Translation - Duane Johnson
English Adaptation - Stormcrow Hayes
Copy Editor - Peter Ahlstrom
Junior Editor - Kara Stambach
Design and Layout - Jose Macasocol, Jr. and Fawn Lau
Cover Design - Christian Lownds

Senior Editor - Nicole Monastirsky
Digital Imaging Manager - Chris Buford
Managing Editor - Lindsey Johnston
Editor-in-Chief - Rob Tokar
VP of Production - Ron Klamert
Publisher - Mike Kiley
President and C.O.O. - John Parker
C.E.O. - Stuart Levy

A **TOKYOPOP** Novel

TOKYOPOP Inc.
5900 Wilshire Blvd. Suite 2000
Los Angeles, CA 90036

E-mail: info@TOKYOPOP.com
Come visit us online at www.TOKYOPOP.com

ISBN: 1-59816-447-3

First TOKYOPOP printing: June 2006
10 9 8 7 6 5 4 3 2 1
Printed in the USA

Character Files

Kite

A Twin Blade with the ability to rewrite data; he is trying to help his friend Orca, who also fell into a coma. He teams up with BlackRose.

BlackRose

A Heavy Blade role-played by Akira Hayami. She only enters The World to determine why her little brother, Fumikazu, fell into a coma.

Chimney

A friendly Blademaster and Nova's partner. His goal is to spring all traps.

Nova

A Heavy Blade partnered with Chimney. He teaches BlackRose the basics of The World.

Mia

A catlike avatar who shouldn't exist. She takes an interest in Kite's bracelet and gives Akira information. She is often seen with Elk, a Wavemaster.

Balmung

Known as one of the "Descendents of Fianna," he completed the The One Sin event along with Orca. He's also trying to find information about Orca's coma and believes Kite might be the cause.

Natsume

A Twin Blade who runs into Kite. She doesn't understand how dangerous this adventure is.

Mistral

A highly inquisitive Wavemaster who likes to collect unusual items. Though she often seems impulsive, she is actually quite level-headed.

History of [The World]

End of the 20th Century

The U.S. Department of Defense develops the ARPANET, which becomes the basis of the Internet. By 1999, almost everyone across the world has access.

Beginning of the 21st Century

As the Internet increases in popularity, classified government information becomes harder to conceal and easier to obtain. Hackers continue to attack networks; cyber crime increases.

2002.10

The United Nations subsystem, WNC, is implemented.

2003.1

WNC winter meeting.

2003.4

A new virus called *Hello, WNC* infects up to ten million users.

2003.12

The Japanese youth who created the *Deadly Flash* virus is sentenced to death.

2004.4

At the WNC spring meeting, the following bills are passed: *Investigation and Research of New Viruses, Technical Security Development Aid,* and *Strengthening Reinforced Penal Regulations of Net Crime.*

2004.8

Emma Weilant dies.

The net poem *Epitaph of Twilight* is lost before it can be completed.

The Swiss Bank's main computer gets hacked, losing more than $84 million.

2005.1

Hacking causes the New York Stock Exchange's prices to hike.

2005.12

On December 24th, *Pluto Kiss* shuts down the Internet; all network computers and communication control systems crash, only to recover 77 minutes later. A 10-year-old elementary school student causes the virus.

2006.1

America's 44th president, Jim Stonecold, resigns.

ALTIMIT OS becomes The World's most commonly used operating system.

2006 Summer

CyberConnect Corporation (CC Corp.) takes over and becomes the foundation for The World.

Harold Hoerwick sells Fragment to CC Corp.

2007.1

The ALTIMIT OS Corporation (head office in San Francisco) establishes 12 overseas affiliation firms.

2007.5

Watarai and Junichiro Tokuoka begin work on the Japanese version of Fragment, which later becomes The World.

ALTIMIT OS' Fragment begins its test play.

2007.7

Fragment becomes the most popular topic among network game users.

2007.10

WNC announces that all computers switch to ALTIMIT OS.

On December 24th, the United Nations names *The Mother Mary's Kiss* an international holiday.

CC Corp. announces the release of Fragment.

2007.11
Beginning of the month

Within the beginning of the first hour, The World receives more than 100,000 orders.

2007.11
End of the month

CC Corp. denies the rumors of discontinuing The World.

2007.12.24

The World's Network Security Declaration President, Alex Coleman, is informed of the start of The World's download sale.

2010

While debugging, Watarai meets with the Vagrant AI. (Story #1, 2nd Character)

Watarai investigates the cat PC. (Story #2, Wotan's Spear, based on *.hack// Sign*)

The second Internet crash, *Pluto Again,* occurs. (Based on the PS2 game)

2011

Watarai leaves CC Corp.

2013

Saki Shibayama takes over as official debugger. (Story #3, Kamui)

Rena Kunisaki purchases The World. (Story #4, Rumor)

2014

.hackers Official Limited Edition Character Exhibition. (Story #5, Firefly, based on .hack// Legend of the Twilight)

BlackRose Sets Foot on The World

Darkness surrounded me, except for the light of the blood-red moon. Something tickled my feet. I looked down to see crimson rose petals. Suddenly, the floral scent strangled me. I struggled to move, to breathe, to escape. I was alone in the wilderness. Then I saw her.

She stood on a distant hillside, her silhouette outlined by the eerie moonlight. I moved toward her, but my body felt sluggish, weighed down. Still, I dragged my feet forward, step by step, inch by miserable inch. I had to talk to her.

I drew closer. I could see her hair swaying in the wind. She stood with her back to me. Slowly, her details were revealed in the crimson moonlight. She wore an evening dress made of silk, but it was tattered and torn. Her arms and legs were covered with wounds. Even so, she was still really beautiful.

I finally stood close enough to touch her. I extended my hand to tap her shoulder, but as I did, a sudden gust of wind scattered a tornado of rose petals through the air. She slowly turned toward me. Blood-streaked tears ran down her face.

I tried to speak, to scream, but no sound escaped my throat as I found myself staring at my own frightening mirror image.

● ⬡ ●

I woke, shaking, my throat dry. I had fallen asleep in the chair next to my brother.

Fumikazu lay in the hospital bed; tubes flowed in and out of every appendage. The only sound he made came from the respirator and the machines that recorded his biorhythms. I reached over and held his hand. Looking at his closed eyelids, I couldn't help but ask, "What happened, little brother? How long are you going to sleep like this?"

I first had the dream after Fumikazu collapsed. Now the nightmare came regularly.

BlackRose Sets Foot on The World

I felt a tear run down my cheek. I turned away from my brother's blank face and stood to leave.

On the bus ride home from the hospital, I looked out the window. Staring at the setting sun, I wondered if Fumikazu would ever again witness such beauty.

I was glad that I'd been able to visit him there in the hospital, to give him what support I could. My afternoons were usually taken up by tennis practice, but the team had taken the day off, so I'd jumped on the bus to see Fumikazu before visiting hours ended.

Come to think of it, the last time I didn't have tennis practice was the day this all began . . .

• ⬡ •

As soon as I'd walked through the front door that day, I could hear Kouta calling our mom from the living room.

"Mama, let's play!"

I found Kouta tugging at the hem of Mom's pants while she took a phone call. I ran over to help.

"Kouta, leave Mom alone while she talks. Why don't you play with me?" I squatted down next to him.

"You wanna draw?" he asked.

"Let's play a game." I had zero artistic talent and hated drawing more than anything.

"Let's draw! I wanna draw something!" he insisted.

"Okay." I sighed. "Go get some paper and crayons."

While he reached for the drawer with the materials, my mom hung up the phone.

"Thanks, Akira. I can take over." She then turned to my little brother. "Kou, you want to draw with Mommy?"

Kouta clung to my leg. "I'll draw with her."

"Come now, Kou. Your sister just got home from school. She needs to change her clothes."

Kouta nodded.

"We'll play after I've changed, okay?"

He reluctantly agreed and I headed for the stairs.

"When you're done, ask Fumikazu to come down, okay?" my mom asked.

I quickly changed and knocked on Fumikazu's door. He didn't answer, so I walked in. He sat in front of his PC with his goggles on.

My little brother loved online games. Lately, he'd been obsessed with something called The World.

BlackRose Sets Foot on The World

"Is that all you ever do? Play video games?" I shouted so he could hear me.

Fumikazu turned from the screen and raised the goggles over his forehead. "This is loads of fun. You should try it!"

"You know I hate role-playing games." I'd tried a few before, but kept giving up after getting stymied by some mystery or other.

"But this one's different from regular RPGs," he protested. "You get to interact with different party members from all over the globe. The World may be virtual, but those people are real!"

I sighed. "Right. And you get to hunt evil monsters and slay dragons and everyone's a hero, right? It's so silly."

"No! You don't get it. There are only *two* heroes—the Descendants of Fianna! They're the only ones who managed to clear the The One Sin event!"

Whose descendants? I didn't understand a thing he said. He might as well have been speaking a different language.

Fumikazu must've picked up on my skepticism, since he returned to his controller and muttered, "Well, you'd have fun if you tried it."

What he'd said did start ringing a few bells. My school friends had been talking about The World lately. Something about someone or other's descendants and fighting with waves and swords . . . since I wasn't into it, though, I hadn't paid much attention when they got on that topic.

"Hey, c'mere!" Fumikazu beckoned me to his monitor. "Let me just show you something!"

"I can't see a thing," I told him.

"Oh. Let me switch off my FMD."

"Your what?"

"The FMD is the Face Mount Display," he explained.

"Oh, you mean your stupid goggles?"

Once he made the switch, I saw a menu appear on the screen. In the topmost window was the Δ symbol followed by three words: Lonely, Corrupt, Spiral.

"What's that?" I asked.

"That's where I go when I enter a gate on the Delta server. Here, I'll let you choose my next destination. You have to fill in the words for the three choices.

"Just any random words?"

"No." He looked annoyed. "They have to be listed in these menus."

BlackRose Sets Foot on The World

He clicked one and a long list of choices scrolled down. "There's three parts—A, B, and C, right?"

"Okay." I nodded.

"Choose one of these words for my first coordinate." Fumikazu deleted the three previous words and highlighted the choices for part A.

"I can choose any of these words?"

"Right. When you put in all three coordinates, it warps you to the corresponding field."

I didn't really see the point, but picking three things from a list was easy enough. I leaned in closer to the monitor and noticed that in the background a boy was wearing a white cape. Was that Fumikazu's character? He looked so much like the real Fumikazu, I couldn't help but laugh.

"What're you laughing at?"

"You, doofus!" I pointed to the character on the display.

"He's an accomplished Wavemaster."

"Wavemaster? What's that?"

Fumikazu looked at me as if I were an idiot. "It's someone who uses magic, like a wizard. But in here, they're called Wavemasters."

" 'Wavemaster' sounds wussy."

"Maybe to you."

"I'd never be a wuss like that."

"Shut up."

"Is that why you want me to play, so you can cast spells on me to make me do your homework?" I jabbed him in the side.

"Stop it! I just think you'd have fun."

"Not as a goofy Wavemaster, though."

"No, I think you'd make a good Heavy Blade. They're warriors, Sis."

"Not interested." I shrugged.

"Why not? I think you'd be cool, chopping off monsters' heads with a big sword."

"Yeah, sure." I returned to the menu he'd opened and pointed to one of the words.

Hidden.

He clicked on it, and the second menu dropped down.

"Okay, choose another. What's next?" he asked.

Fumikazu scrolled slowly down the list of choices. Unlike the first menu, some of the choices had more than one word, but this added bit of variety didn't stop me from beginning to get bored. I selected the next one at random. "Um . . . how about *Forbidden?*"

"Hidden, Forbidden. Sounds promising." He smiled.

Then he clicked open the C group's menu. I knew which choice I wanted as soon as I saw it. "How about Holy Ground for the last one?"

"Perfect! Hidden, Forbidden, *Holy Ground.*"

Looking back on that moment, this was the fateful turning point. If only there were some way I could have known the devastating consequences my choice would soon yield . . . But at the time, we were both equally ignorant.

"That sounds great," Fumikazu said. "I bet there are lots of monsters to kill there."

I remembered Mom waiting for us downstairs. "Mom's gonna kill you if you don't move your butt for dinner."

"Okay, I'll be down in a minute."

The monitor went blank as he drew his goggles, or FMD, or whatever the thing's called, back over his eyes.

I shook my head and went downstairs, thinking of the crazy words I had chosen: Hidden, Forbidden, Holy Ground. I hated to admit it, but they did sound kinda cool.

Downstairs, I found Kouta drawing with his crayons.

"What are you making, Kouta?" I took a look at the paper. There were five vaguely people-shaped blobs drawn in various colors. Our family, I assumed.

Mom came out of the kitchen. "Where's Fumikazu?"

"Uh, finishing up a game. He said he'd be down in a moment."

Then there was a crash and a heavy thud above us. Mom and I exchanged glances.

"Fumikazu?" I called out. "You okay up there?"

Silence was the only reply.

I ran upstairs and threw open his door. Fumikazu lay sprawled out on his back, completely motionless, his legs entangled with his toppled chair, and his controller still tightly grasped in his hand.

"What happened?!" I screamed.

I shook him, but he didn't respond. I tore the goggles off of his head. His eyes were vacant, his pupils rolled back. He didn't move.

"Wake up!" I slapped his cheek. He looked pale.

I ran downstairs, my legs shaking. I tried telling Mom to call an ambulance, but I just sobbed.

BlackRose Sets Foot on The World

"Akira, what happened?!" my mother shouted.

My heart pounded; I couldn't think. I sank to the floor as she ran upstairs.

The sound of the ambulance siren brought me back with a start. I lifted my head and noticed my mother on the verge of tears.

"Akira, you need to get a hold of yourself! I need you to look after Kouta, all right?" A moment later, she was gone.

I listened to the siren as it faded in the distance. Holding Kouta, I staggered upstairs and into Fumikazu's room. My foot accidentally kicked the goggles, which now lay on the floor. Light spilled out from the built-in display.

I set Kouta down and looked through the goggles. I couldn't believe what I saw.

The image looked like it was the interior of a church. But it seemed to me like an evil place. At the altar stood the statue of a girl bound in chains. *This is a game?!* I felt scared.

Suddenly, the image froze and was replaced by the flashing words: SYSTEM ERROR.

I removed the goggles and saw Kouta playfully tapping on the keyboard.

"I'm sorry," Kouta apologized.

"It's okay." I hugged him tightly.

When Mom finally got back home, her face looked stricken with grief as she reported the bad news—Fumikazu was in a coma. It didn't seem possible to me. Had the game caused it, or was there something else wrong with Fumikazu?

Dad was stunned when he heard. We went to bed that night with hardly another word. I couldn't sleep; thoughts of my brother haunted me every second.

● ◆ ●

A bump in the road jostled me back to awareness on the bus ride home from the hospital. I suddenly felt like I had remembered an important clue. Finding Fumikazu unconscious on the floor of his room had driven the details from my memory for a time, but why had I not remembered them until now?

In the days that followed his collapse, I had read everything I could on whether or not video games could cause comas like the one Fumikazu had fallen into. One of

BlackRose Sets Foot on The World

the things I learned about was a condition called PCR, or photoconvulsive response, which occurs when an image is rapidly flashed off and on. It sometimes causes seizures, but only to those susceptible to such things. I found an article that said a program called "Deadly Flash," which exploited the phenomenon, had spread through the net about a year earlier as a sort of sick practical joke. However, there were no cases of it in the past six months. But Fumikazu had been in the middle of a game, so an external program seemed unlikely to be responsible. Besides, the effects of PCR wear off pretty quickly, but Fumikazu wasn't coming out of his coma, so that couldn't be it.

But now as I thought back on those words I had chosen from the game menus—Hidden, Forbidden, Holy Ground—I couldn't escape the feeling that somehow the game, or rather I (since I had chosen the words), had been responsible for putting him into his coma. And ever since he'd collapsed, I'd started having the recurring dream.

And the church I had seen, with its creepy statue . . . suddenly I was reminded of a conversation I'd had with my friends over lunch a month earlier. Shouko's boyfriend Yuuji had brought up The World.

"I heard another ghost appeared. Did you?"

"Yeah, I read it on the BBS," Shouko answered.

"Is that some kind of event?" Miho jumped into the conversation.

"Hey, why don't we meet up at the church tonight?" Yuuji suggested.

"No! It might really be haunted," Shouko replied.

"It's just a game," he countered.

At the time, I'd ignored most of what they were saying. But now the suggestion of a church, a ghost, and what I saw through the goggles swirled around my brain. I realized I would understand better if I went there myself.

I decided to try out The World.

But what if I end up like Fumikazu? My poor parents would be devastated! Maybe I shouldn't go after all. But if I didn't go, I would never learn anything.

Would any of this have happened if I hadn't chosen those words? If he fell into a coma because of something I did, then it was my responsibility to do whatever I could to help him.

When I finally made it home, I went up to my room and sat in front of my computer. I logged on and registered a new account, determined to create my own character. I recalled Fumikazu telling me I would make a good Heavy Blade, so I chose that as my class. Next, I was asked to allocate points among physical and magical offense and defense. Since just swinging a big sword around is all about physical power, I put most of the points into physical offense.

Finally, I was asked to create a character name. She was a girl, so I first thought it should be something graceful. Then I thought of Fumikazu lying there in his hospital bed, and of how little brothers should be able to depend on their big sisters to protect them. And then the dream I kept having again came to my mind, how my other self always wore a jet-black evening gown, surrounded by rose petals. The way she stood there, strong and beautiful though covered with wounds, resonated with me—I was hurting for my brother's sake, but I wanted to be strong and mature despite my pain and the darkness that seemed to be closing in around me.

I made up my mind and typed in the name.

And in that instant, BlackRose took her first steps upon the surface of The World.

Encounter Attack

I was transfixed by the scenery. I stood along a canal; the setting sun turned its waters a fiery orange. Brick and stone houses lined the canal—I noticed strange patterns adorned the walls and doorways. Later, I learned these were called Waves and represented the various elements of power, such as earth, wind, and fire. Someone controlling those powers, like Fumikazu, was called a Wavemaster rather than a "magic user."

Next to me revolved what was called a Chaos Gate, the method of transportation in and out of the field or the other towns. It shimmered with a golden hue.

Around me, avatars talked animatedly. I could see all kinds of other characters as they hurried past. A big suit of green armor loomed before me. I barely had time to look up at the Heavy Axeman when he passed right through me and disappeared into the Chaos Gate. Characters couldn't bump into each other, but his ghostly passing felt creepy. I decided that I should move away from the gate.

But it wasn't as easy as I had thought. It had been years since I held a video game controller; the landscape swirling around me was a dizzying blur. I wouldn't get anywhere unless I learned how to move!

Nearby, players stared.

One of them approached. "Are you a newbie?"

I tried turning in his direction and eventually managed to see who it was. The Heavy Blade standing before me laughed, and beckoned the Blademaster beside him.

"I'm Nova and this is Chimney. Did you just start playing today?"

"Yeah, a few minutes ago."

Silence. It looked like the two of them were talking to each other, but I couldn't hear anything. The quiet made me nervous. I hated these games.

"Do you understand how to move?" Chimney suddenly asked. "If you don't, I'll teach you."

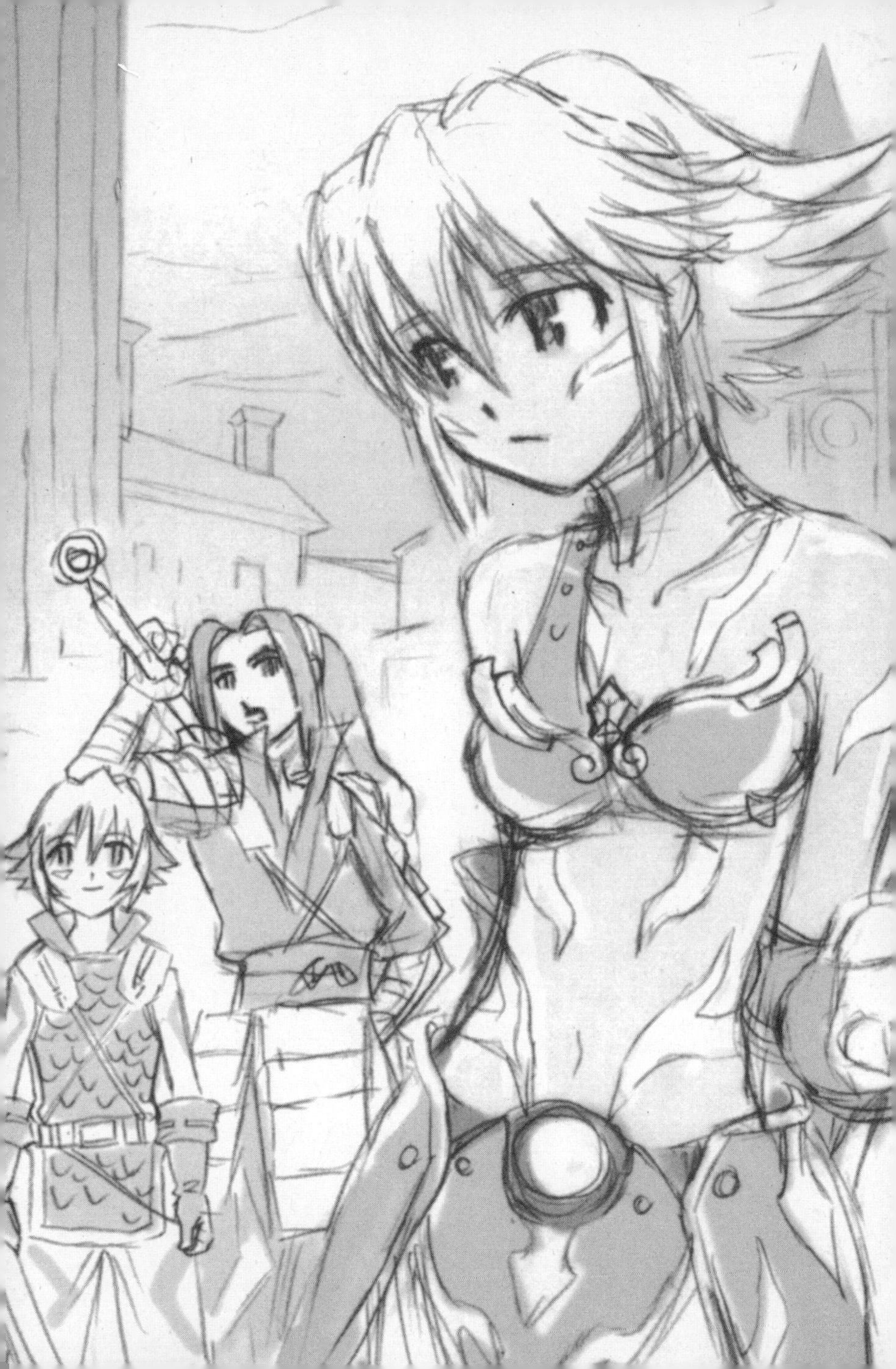

Chimney walked around me in a circle.

"Don't feel nervous. We just want you to get used to The World quickly so you can enjoy it." Nova smiled.

They seemed nice, so I decided to take them up on their offer.

"Uh, yes, please," I replied. "I think I can use any help I can get."

"Then I'll invite you into the party. It'll be easier to teach you that way. Shall we exchange member addresses?"

Member addresses? What was he talking about?

I grabbed the instruction book, but suddenly a window appeared on my screen.

`Nova>> wishes to form a party!`

Not sure what I was getting into, I entered the party.

"Set your voice chat to Party Mode."

"Um . . . okay."

They taught me the different kinds of chats, including how you could talk to just the people in your party, secretly talk to one other person, or talk to everyone around you at once, which was the default.

Nova and Chimney also patiently taught me to maneuver and perform basic commands. After I managed the basics, I walked clumsily through the town. I'd been playing for roughly an hour when we approached the edge of the canal.

"So why did you start playing The World?" asked Chimney.

"You shouldn't ask questions like that!" Nova scolded.

"Why not?"

"It's rude."

"Okay, sorry," Chimney apologized.

"Sure," I answered.

Nova changed the subject. "I'd like to head out into the field and fight some monsters. Sorry, we need to get going."

"Is it that time already?" asked Chimney.

"We made prior arrangements. Let's play again sometime!" Nova offered.

"See you later!" Chimney added cheerily.

I used the motion commands they taught me and bowed to them. "Thanks for your help!"

"E-mail me if there's anything you don't understand, all right? See ya," Nova said.

"Oh, hey. Once you're used to things, you might want to check out Hidden, Forbidden, Holy Ground."

How does he know about that place?!

"There's nothing in that field. No monsters show up, so it's safe," Chimney added.

They waved and left. Their status icons disappeared from the display.

I couldn't get Chimney's last words out of my head. *How could Hidden, Forbidden, Holy Ground be safe?!*

Using my new skills, I turned toward the Chaos Gate. Even though it was only a game, my legs felt heavy.

If it's safe, then what happened to Fumikazu?! I had a feeling there was some unseen evil lurking there. In any case, all I could do was go there myself. Nothing would be accomplished if I didn't. It was just a game, right?

I kept telling myself that there was nothing to be afraid of, but . . .

Kouta's crying brought me back to the real world. I took off the goggles and turned just as Kouta ran into the room. I caught hold of him. "What's the matter?"

Tears stained his cheeks. "Mommy's scary. I wanna stay with you."

"I'm busy right now."

"Akira, would you mind taking care of Kouta?" Mom's voice floated up from downstairs. She sounded weak and shaky. Ever since my brother's collapse, she had trouble dealing with the rest of the family, especially the needs of a five-year-old. "Akira, did you hear me?"

"Okay, Mom." *How could I refuse?*

I logged out and carried Kouta downstairs. He stayed by my side all night, until we finally fell asleep on the couch watching videos.

● ⬡ ●

The dream again.

I found myself wandering through the same savage wilderness, headed toward the same distant figure. Again, I dragged my heavy feet until I reached her. Once more, I extended my hand. But this time the petals didn't swirl up in a whirlwind.

This time she spoke. "Welcome."

She slowly turned. She held a massive golden sword. She turned its hilt to me and held it out.

"What's this?" It was the first time I'd ever spoken in the dream.

"Don't . . ." she began, but the rest of her words were too quiet for me to make out. A soft breeze swayed the hem of her torn dress.

I took the hilt in my hand, and she released it into my grasp. The sword was so heavy that I had to grab it with both hands. Then she smiled at me, and the familiar gust of wind kicked up the rose petals. Within the dancing petals so thick they almost blocked my view, her smile stayed fixed on me until I awoke.

She was wounded, all alone in the dark, and I still didn't know why. *But perhaps,* I thought, *her courageous resolve in this strange place actually represents the kind of person I want to be.*

If that's the case, how could I be like her, braving the darkness without hesitation?

● ⬡ ●

By the next day, my resolve had abandoned me.

Despite my desire to go directly to the field, I was scared. BlackRose wandered in circles around the Chaos

Gate. as I just sat there and sighed. I must have looked completely insane.

A short Twin Blade wearing bright green clothing and a large hat that covered his blue hair stepped through the gate. Noticing that I was looking him over, he eyed me back for a moment and then said, "What? What is it? You got something to say?"

"No," I said, surprised.

The Twin Blade backed off. "Oh, I get it. You're a newbie, aren't you? I might have guessed. Listen, in case you're not aware of it, you're being very rude. It's impolite to stare like that. You have to understand, it's the same as the real world. Don't stare."

I didn't want to be looked down upon as a newbie or a fool, but of course, I ended up staring at him longer before turning and running away.

"What is up with you anyway?" the Twin Blade called.

"You don't have to be so mean," I shouted back, and then ran into town.

I kept running through the streets and down the alleys. Whenever something irritated me in real life, I'd jog. Running made me feel like I was driving out all the negative energy of my body and releasing it into the wind. But I couldn't feel wind in a game, so running here wasn't helping nearly as much as I wished.

I pictured Fumikazu's face as he lay in the hospital, then I was reminded of my dream: BlackRose smiling after handing me the golden sword. I realized it was time to stop running. I spun on my heel and made my way back to the Chaos Gate.

The gate shimmered before my eyes. I thought about entering, but now it was the face of that Twin Blade that I couldn't get out of my head. *Does he hate me? Probably. I shouldn't have acted so crazy.* I wanted someone to go with me, so I wouldn't have to go alone. I waited beside the gate to see if he reappeared.

But how should I talk to him if he does? It would sound weird if I asked him to go with me. Why did I want to invite *him*, anyway? If I wanted company, I could ask Chimney and Nova.

As I waited indecisively, the Twin Blade reappeared. He walked past me toward the gate.

"Wait!"

He turned in my direction.

"Look, I'm sorry for the way I acted before, but I know some interesting words. If you come with me, I'll let you in on them." It was a gamble. But I had a feeling he'd bite.

"Words?"

"Yeah, you know, for the gate," I replied.

"Oh. You mean a destination."

"Yeah."

He stood silent for a moment. He must have been thinking about my offer.

"Will you answer already?!" I cried.

"Sure, let's do it."

I sent him my member address and we formed a party. When his stats appeared on my screen, I saw his name was Kite. I could also see that he must've been almost as new to the game as me. So why did he act like such a know-it-all?

"Where are we going?" he asked.

"The words are Hidden, Forbidden, Holy Ground."

"Let's go!"

I entered the destination on the same menu Fumikazu had shown me.

Hidden, Forbidden, Holy Ground. *Is this the place?* My heart filled with uncertainty.

"Wow, look at this!" Kite said as we arrived.

A large stone building towered before us. Surrounding it was a patchy bank of clouds. It was dusk. There was nothing else.

Maybe I was wrong about this location.

Kite looked at me as I peered around.

"Nothing here. Let's go to that building!" Kite turned and ran. I followed.

The building wasn't that far. A large door stood open on one side. We cautiously stepped through.

Once I saw what was inside, my eyes widened. There was no mistake. This was the very place that I had seen on the night Fumikazu collapsed. The statue of the bound girl was there at the altar.

"Hey." I pointed to the statue. "What *is* that thing?"

Suddenly, there was a flicker of movement from the side, and I turned to see what looked like a skinny (and very ugly) dwarf. He stepped out from a hidden alcove to advance on us, his claws raised and fangs bared.

"Aaah! Stay back!" I shouted as I raised my sword shakily. Then I realized I didn't know how to fight in the game. Were there special commands or something?

Encounter Attack

While groping for the manual with one hand, I randomly mashed the controller buttons with the other. I apparently got something right, because my sword swung down and made contact. A small icon appeared over the monster as it collapsed and disintegrated. It read: 70 EXP.

"It was just a wimpy goblin." Kite gestured with one of his Twin Blades at the space the monster had occupied. "You didn't even need my help, did you?"

"Uh, yeah. I handled it."

I doubt Kite bought my tough act, but he just turned and walked toward the statue. I followed closely behind, my heart pounding as he examined the artwork carefully.

The statue girl had eight chains binding her, one on each of her wrists, elbows, and knees, as well as around her hips and neck. It didn't look to me like she was *enshrined* here in this church . . . She was *imprisoned*.

"She looks so sad," I muttered.

Kite leaned forward to look at something engraved on the statue's pedestal.

"What's it say?" I asked.

"*Skeith, Innis, Magus.* I can't read anything after that. The inscription's faded."

"What do you think it means? Are those some kind of names?"

Kite just shrugged and frowned at the faint letters.

I waited in silence while he continued to study the inscription. I thought about this stranger who had agreed to come here with me. I wondered who he was in real life. Either way, I had the impression that he was a good guy. I wondered if I should tell him the real reason I came here.

Fumikazu . . . should I? I decided I could at least try.

"You're nicer than I thought. I mean, you didn't get too mad at me after we first met, and you agreed to come here when you knew I was new to the game. But the real reason I'm—"

The door opened behind us. We both turned in surprise.

"Hey! What are you doing?!" demanded the Blademaster. He strode past the threshold.

Unlike any character I'd seen before, a pair of gorgeous white wings extended from his blue and silver armor. Silver hair framed his angry face as he stared us down.

I wanted to say it was none of his business, but he looked mad enough to kill me!

"What about you, huh?!" Kite defended.

"There's no time to explain! It's too dangerous here!" the knight shouted.

"What?" Kite said.

"I'm telling you to get out!"

He suddenly charged. A name appeared above his avatar: Balmung.

"Wh-what're you talking about?" I stammered.

But before I could finish speaking, the screen went haywire; the color inverted to a negative image, and a strange noise erupted in my earphones. Above us, part of the ceiling distorted and then warped into a hole. It opened ever wider, until it expelled a large monster. The creature was headless, yet it carried a skull in its right hand and brandished a sword menacingly in its left.

"Leave here at once!" Balmung shouted to us once more, then leapt at the monster.

With an overhead flash of silver from the knight, the creature fell to its knees and turned black. The Blademaster had defeated it in a single blow.

I heaved a sigh of relief, but then the screeching sound erupted again. The screen colors inverted for a moment, as

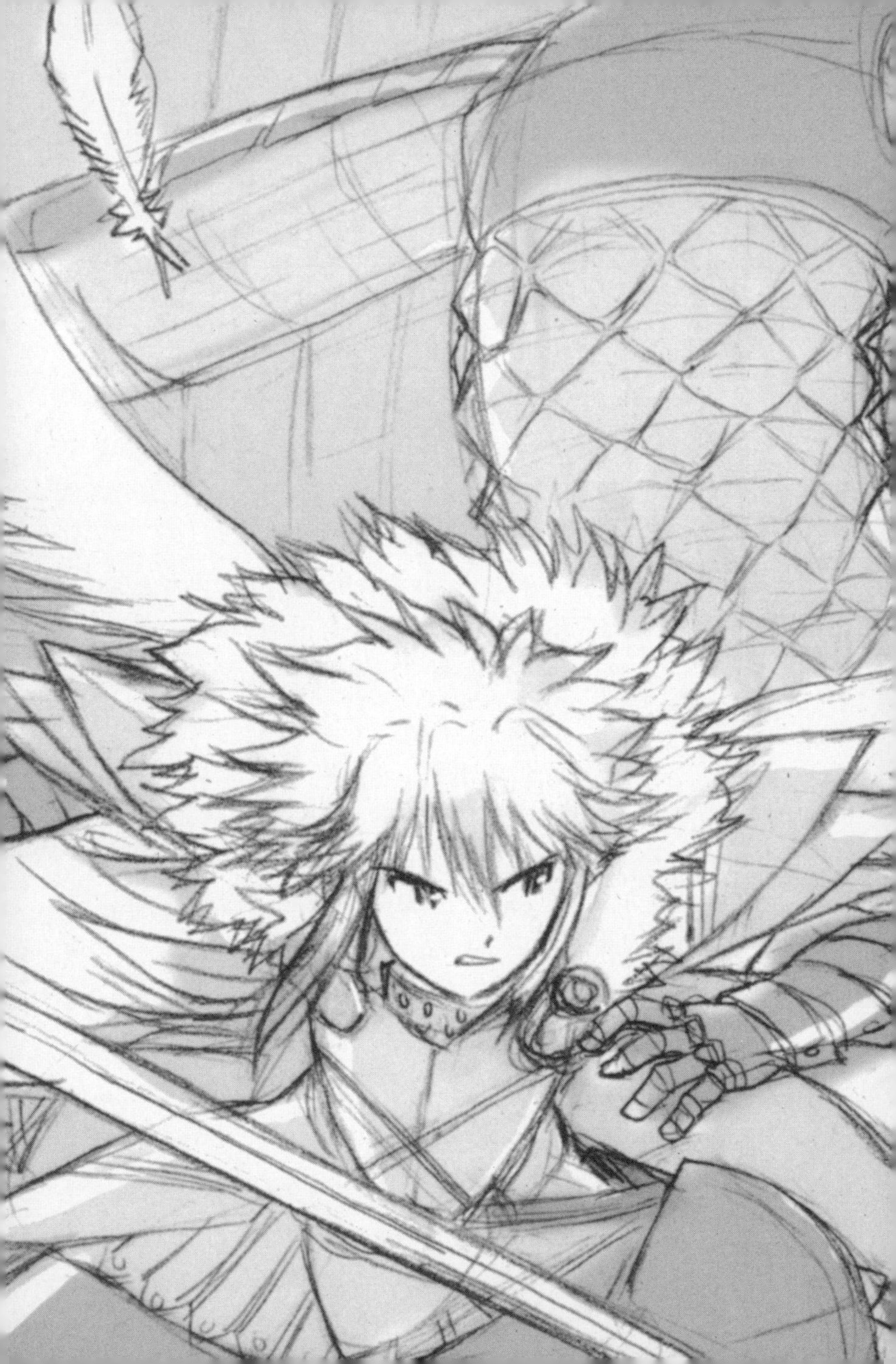

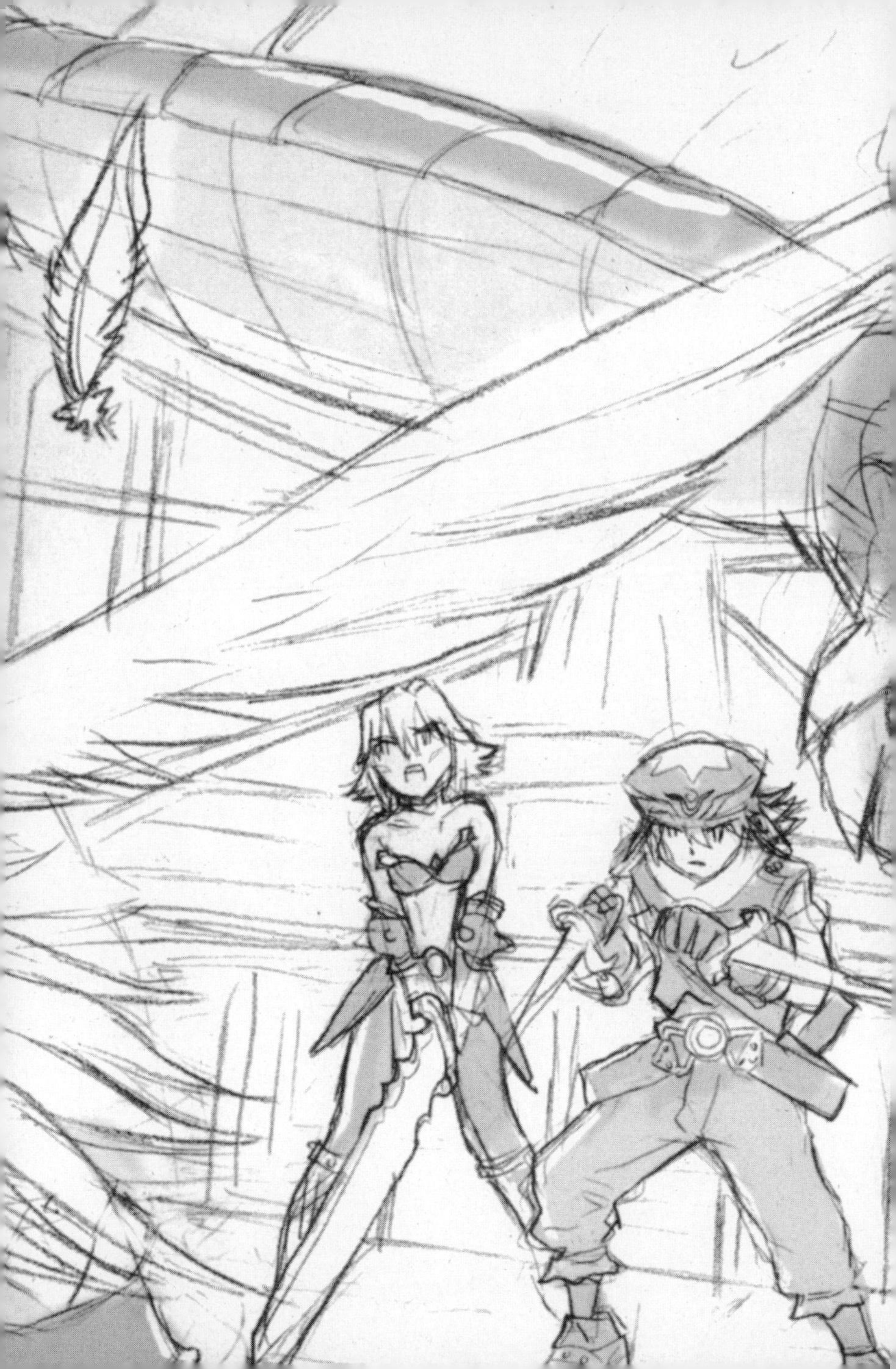

a strange violet field enveloped the body of the monster. Its color returned and the creature, now covered in patchy lines like violet lightning, stood and let out a roar.

Balmung held his ground.

"This one as well," he muttered as he prepared his attack.

Is this part of some kind of event?

"Why isn't that thing dead?" demanded Kite. "What's going on? Why is it glowing like that?"

"It's a Data Bug!" Balmung shouted. "A virus has rewritten its parameters—it has an infinite number of hit points!"

That meant it couldn't be defeated! *Impossible!*

I stared at the monster before me, my throat parched. "This must be the one!" I cried. *Could this creature—or rather, this Data Bug—have attacked Fumikazu?* I was sure he'd fought it bravely, while his own hit points slowly diminished.

If that was true, then it was my fault. *I chose his destination. I brought him here.*

A wash of emotions ran over me: regret, anger, grief, and despair. I brandished my sword.

"I'll kill you!" I cried as I charged.

Balmung shouted behind me, but I couldn't hear what he said.

I slashed at the monster. I knew I couldn't defeat it, but my rage had overtaken me.

"Didn't you hear me?!" Balmung appeared by my side, continuing his attack. His voice sounded bitter; he knew it was impossible to win.

"I can't run away!" I slashed the monster again and again—to no avail. "Fumikazu!" I shouted his name like a war cry.

Suddenly, a dazzling light speared the monster from somewhere behind me. The creature took a direct hit, and the patchy lines of lightning vanished.

Balmung slashed again, and it collapsed to the ground, dead. This time it disappeared, like all defeated monsters should.

"But h-how . . . ?" Balmung stammered, confused.

I suddenly felt weak and tired; the strength drained from my own tense body. I sank back into my chair.

Balmung turned toward Kite. "Now I understand," he declared coldly. "Look at you. You're just as bad as the virus that caused this. To think that I was saved by *you!*"

What is he talking about?

"No, it's not me. I mean . . . I don't even know——" Kite tried to explain.

"Do not lie to me!" Balmung stood directly before Kite. I couldn't understand why he was so angry.

"What's going on?!" I shouted.

"Recently, many places in The World have been damaged by a strange virus. Anyone spreading the virus shall receive no mercy!" Balmung cried out in anger. "I did not expect to find the one responsible so soon."

"But I didn't do anything," Kite bleated.

Balmung raised his sword.

How could Kite be responsible? It doesn't make sense. But he somehow managed to defeat the monster with one magical strike. What did he do?

"Defend yourself," demanded Balmung.

"I won't! There's no reason to fight!"

"I've got a damn good reason! Draw!" The larger Blademaster advanced.

"I don't want to fight," Kite insisted. "I just——"

I was furious. "What is the *matter* with you?!" I yelled at Balmung. "That's hardly the way to talk to someone who just saved your life!" I charged toward him; he dodged me with a quick sidestep.

The three of us faced each other down. Finally, Balmung drew back a pace and sheathed his sword.

"I still don't trust you," he said, glaring at each of us in turn. "I just require the time to think this through." He turned and walked toward the door. "But if I find out that you are indeed in league with the hackers, I *will* destroy you!" Then he was gone.

I looked at Kite and noticed for the first time that his clothing had changed from bright green to a burning orange-red. Strange designs coiled around the clothes.

"What happened to your outfit?" I asked. "And was that some kind of magic you used to defeat that monster?"

Kite shrugged dejectedly. "I don't know."

Somehow, Kite's magic had rendered the creature vulnerable to Balmung's final strike. *But how did he do it?* The virus had been able to rewrite the monster's data to make it invincible, but Kite's skill rewrote the Data Bug's parameters again, returning it to an ordinary monster.

But he's just a newbie like me! Unless there was something to what Balmung said . . . I looked at Kite more closely and realized that the color of his clothes wasn't the only thing that had changed: a bracelet had appeared on his right arm.

Noticing that I stared at the bracelet, Kite touched it with his left hand. He stood silently for a long time. When he finally spoke, his voice was filled with sorrow, like a lost child with no hope of finding his home. "Orca fell into a coma."

I almost dropped the controller. *A coma?* My heartbeat thundered furiously in my ears.

Kite told me his story. He was a newbie, as his level indicated. He'd just started playing the game after being invited by his friend Orca. It seems Orca had garnered quite a reputation in The World as a Blademaster. He was even legendary. He'd promised Kite to show him the ropes, but the first time Kite went with him to a field, they witnessed a girl being chased by a monster unlike anything Orca had ever seen.

The girl tried to give Orca something resembling a book, but the monster jumped between them and attacked. Eventually, its onslaught was too much for Orca. It killed him. Normally when characters died in The World, a death icon flashed over their heads and they disappeared, but when

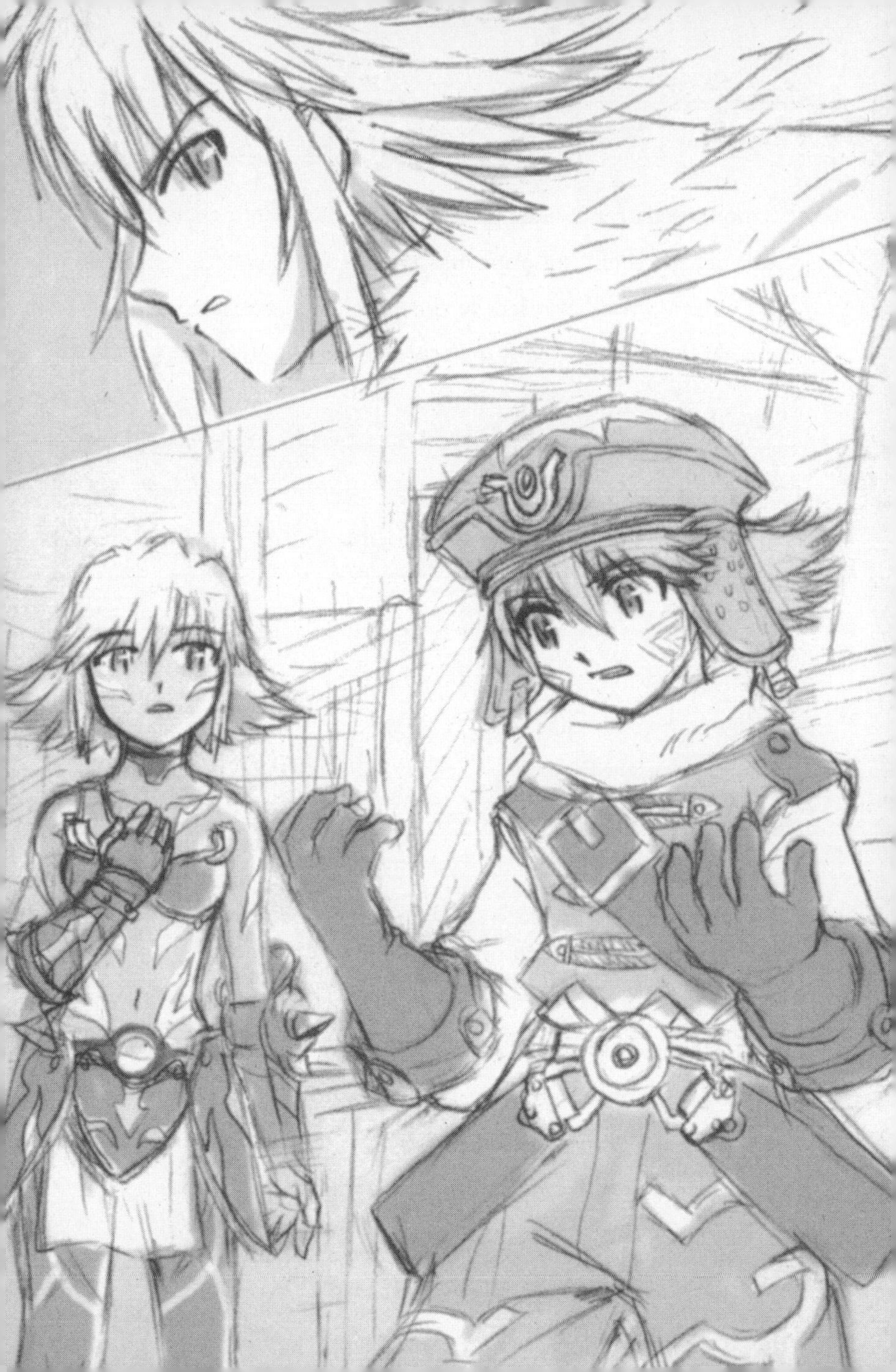

this monster defeated Orca, Orca was pierced by a mysterious light and his character data disassembled into pieces. Or at least, that's what I understood—Kite's explanation was a little garbled. He was very emotional when he talked about it.

Kite was also nearly killed by the creature, but just before it struck, some kind of staff fell from the sky and warped him to another field. His life had been saved, but he wasn't sure why.

Afterward, Kite tried contacting his friend, but he didn't respond. It wasn't until later that he learned that Orca had fallen into a coma.

My head swam.

My second day of playing, and already I've met someone in the same predicament.

Kite continued his story. "When Balmung was fighting the Data Bug monster here, I thought he might end up like Orca did, so I desperately wanted to do something to stop it. Suddenly it was like I heard a voice . . . I think it was the girl who we saw being chased, the one who tried to give a book to Orca. I think she somehow gave me the skill that helped us defeat the Data Bug."

So the same power that can put someone into a coma can also defeat the monsters that caused it?

"I don't really understand this power or what she wanted Orca to do with it. I only know that it's mine now and I want to use it to save Orca, but . . ." he paused, trying to collect himself. "But I don't know how."

I understood his anguish and helplessness. But it didn't seem like something I could put into words. All I could do was look at him and nod.

We returned in silence to the Delta server root town, Mac•Anu. As always, the chaos gate was revolving, but the pretty round shape of the gate now looked a little distorted to me. The World was a beautiful place, but there was darkness lurking in its depths.

At least I finally had some clues, but I needed time to absorb everything, so I told Kite I needed to sleep and logged out. As I left, I could feel his sad eyes staring at me.

• ⬡ •

I shivered. Fumikasu's room was cold. Even though I'd left The World, what I'd seen had been too vivid to easily forget. My arm felt strangely sluggish, like I'd been holding a heavy sword in real life. It reminded me of the huge sword I'd been given in my dream. Somehow, the muscle memory of my grip on the weapon linked the game with the real world.

Stretching, I got up from my chair and decided to check on Hana, Fumikazu's pet.

I quietly entered Fumikazu's room. Opening the prairie dog pen, I took Hana from her cage, then sat down in front of the window and held her in my lap.

A year earlier, there had been a ban on these small animals, but it was lifted right before my brother decided to buy a pet with his birthday money.

When Fumikazu had first gotten her, I was not amused—she reminded me too much of a big rat. But I'd grown used to the prairie dog, and now I enjoyed these quiet moments, sitting together in the darkness.

Her eyelids drooped as I petted her.

"What just happened? That was just a game, wasn't it?" I mumbled. Hana just chirped at me.

I watched the rain slide down the window and wondered if I could continue going to The World.

Would I end up like Fumikazu? If Kite hadn't used his skill, I could have been lying unconscious right now.

I didn't have enough information. Nor was I powerful enough.

Hana squirmed in my hands. I realized I was holding her too tightly. "Sorry," I said, petting her head to make amends.

I gazed at our family portrait that sat on top of Fumikazu's desk. Kind Fumikazu . . . he always believed in everyone. That sometimes got him into trouble, but even if he got tricked, he wouldn't give up on people.

I decided that I would believe in Kite.

I returned Hana to her cage and fed her. "You be sure to eat," I told her. (She'd been eating less since Fumikazu's collapse.) I went to my room and decided to e-mail Kite. I quickly typed a short message:

```
I don't really understand what
happened, but I believe your story. I'm
very busy with school, but I'd like to
help with your quest. Please contact
me when you want to continue.
```

I hit "send" and then felt a pang of regret. The doubts returned, but then I realized that I was just being neurotic.

I wished I weren't so scared. I wanted to be strong and courageous—like BlackRose. My other self, who lived in The World. She wouldn't complain, no matter what.

A Bolt from the Blue

I held Fumikazu's delicate hand as I told him about the previous night's adventure. I told him about Orca, so he would know that he wasn't alone and that I was trying to help him any way I could.

Sifting through what had happened, I felt like I had made some progress, but I wasn't sure what any of it meant. Everything was still too scattered, and it left me feeling confused. And yet I also felt like I was on the right track. It definitely was reassuring to find an ally like Kite—someone who was after the same goal.

But if only I'd never suggested those words to Fumikazu . . . "It's my fault you're here," I told my brother. "I'm so sorry."

I squeezed his hand. Even when I tried not to think about it, my guilt weighed heavily on my mind.

• ⬢ •

When I got home, I fired up my PC right away. The familiar *ding* signaled new mail; there were two messages. One was from the CyberConnect Corporation, so I assumed it was registration confirmation or the like, and the other was from Kite. I quickly opened it.

Thanks. Hope to see you around again.

He sounded so indifferent. *Maybe I shouldn't have e-mailed him after all,* I thought, but before I could dwell on it, I heard Mom call me downstairs for dinner.

We'd been eating late recently because Mom would visit Fumikazu in the hospital. In fact, every aspect of life around the house had changed since Fumikazu's collapse. Gone was the dinner table banter, replaced instead by an awkward adherence to ritual politeness. Kouta's complaints about whatever food was "yucky" instead of "yummy" was the only attempt at conversation.

In the past, Mom had never allowed the TV on during dinner, but now no one bothered to turn it off. Often, the terrible sounds of a sitcom's laugh track were all we had to break the mood, but they usually just made the oppressive silence that much worse.

I sat down, my guilt welling up again as I looked at my parents' somber expressions. No one would feel this way if I hadn't chosen that stupid destination, those fateful words.

I wasn't hungry, but I knew Mom would yell if I didn't eat. I put the rice bowl to my mouth and shoveled it in.

Mom gasped. "Akira, stop eating like that. Hisashi, say something to her."

Dad looked at me, but remained quiet. I decided to start a conversation to see if I could lighten the mood.

"They're going to announce who's first string on the tennis team soon. I have to keep my strength up." I rolled up my sleeve and flexed my bicep.

Dad smiled. "You'll knock 'em dead. You've always had good reflexes."

"I'm like you, Dad. Good at sports, bad at studying." I forced myself to smile.

"What do you mean, bad at studying? I'm a school teacher, you know," he said, proudly sticking his chest out.

"Yeah, a *gym* teacher."

Kouta giggled.

"Even a gym teacher has to earn a college degree, and you don't get one without studying," Dad reminded me.

"Yeah, but you hated it, didn't you?"

"Well . . ."

"See!" I said triumphantly. But Dad looked wounded instead of treating it as plain teasing. He turned back to his food.

The table fell silent. I tried not to let my smile fade, but I had nothing else to say. *This sucks.*

"Mommy, I've gotta go potty." Kouta tugged on Mom's sleeve.

"Okay."

Mom and Kouta left the dining room. Dad looked over his shoulder as if checking to make sure they were out of earshot, then turned and looked at me. It made me feel nervous for some reason.

"Akira," he said softly. "I'm sorry."

"Huh?"

"You don't have to force yourself to be cheerful just because you're the big sister."

He noticed. "I'm not forcing anything," I insisted.

He smiled back and we finished eating in silence.

When I got up to clear the dishes, I heard him quietly say, "Your dad has to be stronger, too."

I sat in front of the computer, unable to move. I was suddenly afraid to go back to The World. *What if I end up in a coma just like Fumikazu?* My family would no doubt crack under the strain.

Feeling paralyzed, I realized there was no way I could go into the game today.

I returned the controller to the desk, removed the goggles, and stretched out on my bed. I knew there was a lot I'd be able to learn from the game, but I stood to lose a lot as well. With these conflicting thoughts racing through my mind, I fell asleep.

I didn't have any dreams that night. I almost felt disappointed. Maybe my mirror image in the dream world had fulfilled her duty now that she'd given me the golden sword.

 • ◆ •

"Check it! This time I've got proof," Yuuji said proudly. He approached Risa, Shouko, Miho, and me while we ate lunch the next day.

"You mean the game again?" Shouko pouted. Lately, it seemed like all Yuuji talked about during lunch was gaming.

"Listen, babe, I got on the 'net this morning and read a new thread about ghosts. They swear it's the real thing. Let's go check it out tonight!"

Ghosts? I had to ask, "Do you know an area where ghosts appear?"

Everyone turned and looked at me in surprise.

"Don't tell me *you're* playing The World, Hayami?"

"No. I just can't help being a little interested . . . I mean, I've heard you guys talk about it so much, of course

A Bolt from the Blue

I've caught on to a few things!" I couldn't tell them I had logged on to their game; they might want to join me. Knowing the dangers I faced and the fact that I was searching for the source of the virus, I couldn't endanger my friends.

Besides, they were used to playing for fun. I didn't want to waste time being dragged on silly adventures when I had a real goal to achieve.

"Yeah, could you see Akira playing games?" Miho joked.

"Not at all. She's just not the type."

"Though I have to admit, it would be fun to play together," added Shouko.

"Are you kidding?!" Risa scolded. "You should see Akira in tennis practice! She's totally dedicated to working on her backhand and her serve. She doesn't have time to waste on computer games. In fact, she might even make first string!"

"Risa . . ." I said. "I really don't think that's likely . . ."

I was glad Risa had bailed me out, but . . . *first string? Me?* Risa was on the team too—we'd been friends since elementary school, and she'd been the one who'd convinced *me* to try out for tennis—so she knew as well as I did that there were only five spots and eight juniors; there was no way a freshman like me would get picked.

"Whoa, don't take me so seriously," Risa backpedaled. "It was just a joke."

I sat back. *Of course she was kidding.* I should have realized that immediately and played along. But to me, it wasn't a joke. I knew there was no chance of me making first string, but in my heart, I *really* wanted it.

Though now, what I wanted most in the world was for Fumikazu to recover.

"Anyway," Risa continued to the others, "Akira's totally the outdoorsy type. I just can't see her sitting for hours, cooped up in her room, playing video games!"

If only they knew . . .

●　◆　⬡

After tennis practice ended that afternoon, the coach gathered everyone together. It was pretty obvious what for; standing behind the coach, the upperclassman manager, Asaoka, was holding what had to be the first-string uniforms. Risa and I stood together nervously with the other freshmen.

A Bolt from the Blue

"After paying close attention to your practices up to this point, I'm ready to announce the players for this fall's tournament," the coach said. "If your name is called, please come forward to get your uniform."

The coach rummaged in his pocket for a crumpled memo and handed it to our captain. "Read it, Koura."

"Yes, sir."

My heart was beating fast, even though I knew there was no hope.

"First, in singles, Akira Hayami."

My heart stopped. *Did he just say . . . ?*

"Hayami! Respond!" shouted the coach.

"Yes, sir!" I stood at attention.

"Get your uniform."

I stole a glance at Risa, who looked as shocked as I probably did, then timidly stepped forward and took a uniform from Asaoka. My hands were shaking.

The uniform itself was old and nearly threadbare, but I didn't care. I had actually made it!

"I'm glad you were chosen," Asaoka whispered to me, smiling. "You're always at practice before everyone else to help set up, and you've shown the most dedication."

I was grateful she'd noticed.

"You deserve it. Kick some butt, Hayami."

She let out a little giggle, but tried to keep it quiet; I didn't think she wanted the juniors to hear. I liked Asaoka. She wasn't really the athletic type—to me, she seemed more suited for academic clubs, but she was Captain Koura's childhood friend, so she got the position. And she did a good job keeping things organized.

I took the uniform and returned to my spot next to the stunned Risa. My legs trembled with excitement. I didn't even hear the names that were called for the two doubles teams.

"That's all. Dismissed!"

As the other girls shuffled off to the locker room, the freshmen gathered around me, chattering excitedly. I was still a bit dazed, but Risa had obviously recovered—she tackled me.

"Akira!" she cried. "Congrats!"

I hugged her back. "Are you sure I'm not dreaming?" I asked.

The other freshmen congratulated me as well. "Good luck, Hayami!"

"I'll do my best!" I promised. "Now I'd better practice twice as hard!"

It was finally settling in. Halfway through cleanup, I couldn't hold back the excitement any longer and did a little victory dance. When I turned around, though, the coach was watching. My face felt like a furnace.

"Are you finished?" he said.

I somehow managed not to die on the spot. "Y-yes, sir."

He smiled. "I'm glad to have you on the team. I have high hopes for you, Hayami! Good luck!" He walked off the court.

He has high hopes for me, I thought. And reality set in. As first string, it would be my duty to dedicate all my effort to the team. *But doesn't Fumikazu deserve all my effort as well?*

● ◆ ●

That night at dinner, I saw smiles on my parents' faces for the first time in a long while.

Dad said, "That's my girl!" and Mom was really happy for me. Caught up in the mood, even Kouta giggled. It was so good to see them almost back to normal.

I relaxed so much that I almost wept with joy . . . but I was desperate not to let anyone see me cry.

As I sat down at the computer that night, my doubts from the previous day nagged at me again, but I already knew where my responsibilities lay. Still, it was nearly midnight before I logged on.

I searched to see if Kite was online, but if he was, he didn't reply to my e-mails. It was late and I had no idea whether the real-life Kite would be awake. I realized that I didn't even have any clue about what he was like in real life, such as how old he was or anything like that.

I walked along Mac•Anu's canal, pondering what to do, when my reverie was interrupted.

"Heyyyyyy!"

I turned to see Chimney running toward me, waving. Behind him, Nova walked along more leisurely.

They immediately invited me to join their party and I agreed. The game's party chat mechanism made conversation easier.

"Long time." Chimney ran circles around me the way he had when we'd first met.

"It's only been three days." I smiled.

"That's a long time to me!"

I guess three days is a long time to people who do this every day.

"Your e-mail said you wanted to ask us something?" Nova interrupted.

"Yeah. I heard you talking the other day about a place where monsters don't show up."

"Yeah? You mean the church, right?"

"Yes."

"Yeah, there's nothing there. It's just decoration, which makes it a good place to practice your skills until you become proficient. Most players who've been at this awhile know it's empty."

"And you say things like monsters never show up? Ever?" I pressed.

"What do you mean by '*like* monsters?' "

"Um . . ." I didn't want to tell them about the Data Bug.

Chimney tsked. "You weren't scared of the creepy old church, were you, BlackRose?"

"No, it's not that."

"Did something happen?" asked Nova.

"No, nothing happened."

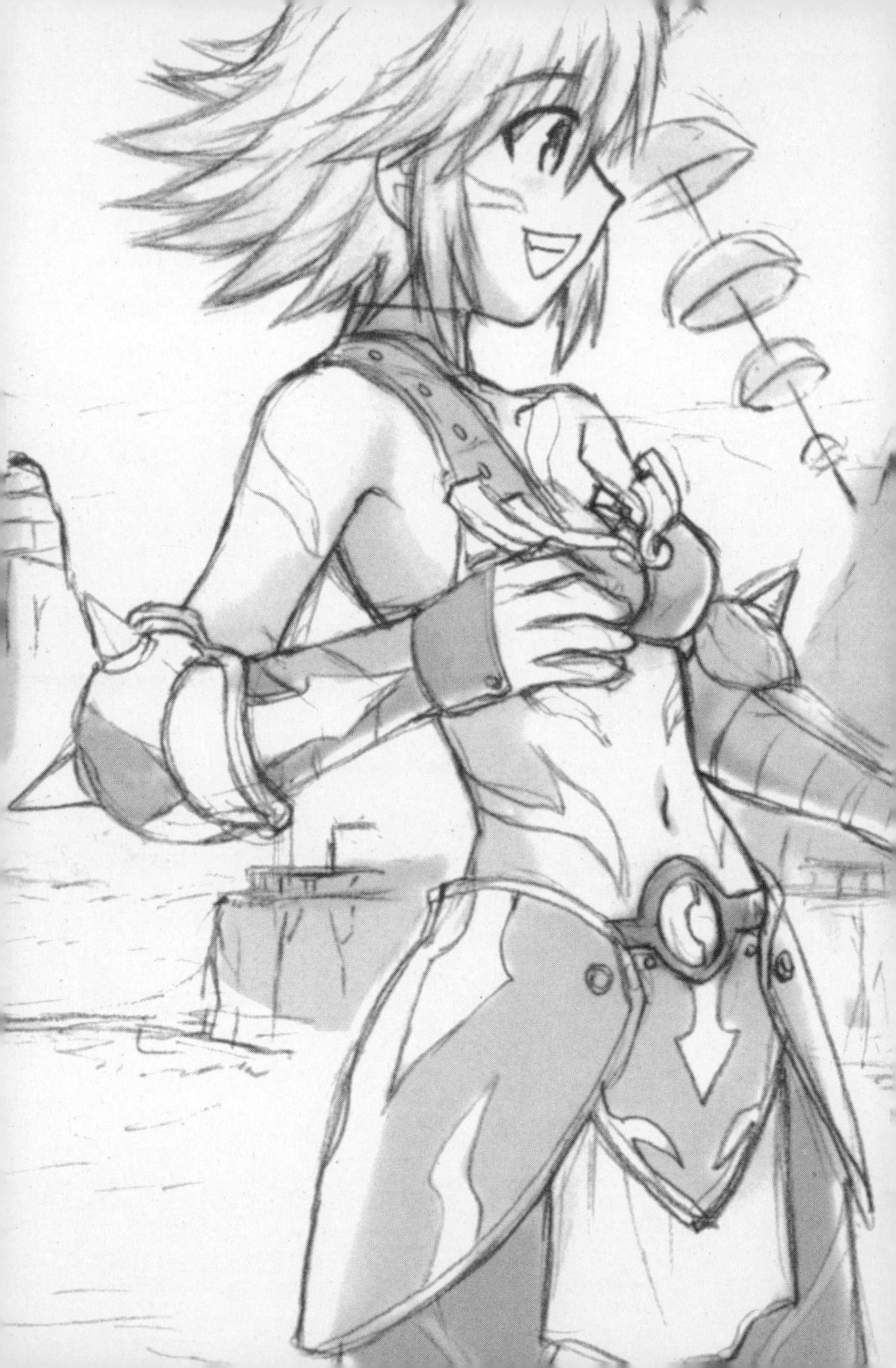

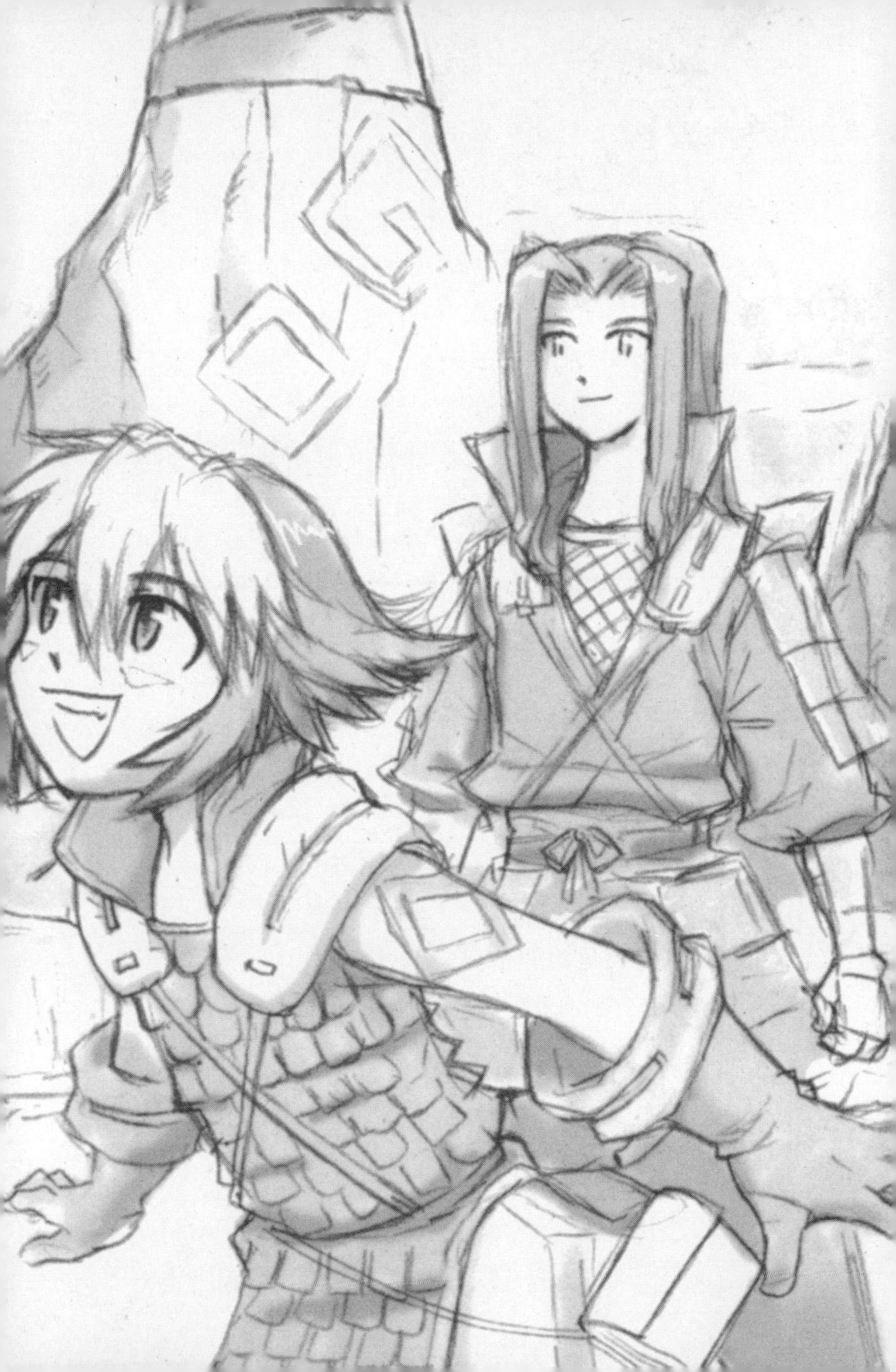

"Why don't we all go together? Chimney and I aren't doing anything, and it's been awhile since I've visited. You wanna go?"

I didn't want to risk running into the creature again. I couldn't deal with it by myself, but I didn't want to get them tangled up in this mess. *How can I dissuade them?* "Uh, no, that's okay."

"No? Then how about we go somewhere else? Have you ever been to that Expansive, Haunted, Sea of Sand place that people are talking about?" Chimney asked.

I was glad he'd changed the subject.

"That place might work," Nova agreed. "The area level's not too high. I think they just finished designing it, so it'll be fresh for all of us."

I had read on the BBS that a mysterious girl had been spotted there. *Could it be the girl Kite mentioned?*

I was a bit uneasy, but I also wanted to check it out. "Okay, that works," I agreed.

"Excellent decision!"

"Let's go right away. Is this your first combat?"

I couldn't tell them I'd fought the other day, so I just nodded.

"Then we'll teach you about combat, too."

"Thanks."

We arrived in a desert region littered with gigantic snail shells (large enough to live inside), and the occasional beached starfish (the size of a truck). The area had apparently been designed to resemble a dried-up ocean.

"Oh, goody, there are lots of them," muttered Chimney.

"Lots of what?" I asked.

"Magic portals," Nova said as he pointed to a big, yellow, spinning sphere with hand-drawn designs specific to the region.

"If you get close to the yellow thing, it invokes a magic portal. Try it out, BlackRose."

I walked closer. The sphere was roughly twice my height. The instant my avatar stood close enough to touch it, the patterns on its surface unraveled and burst open. A blue treasure box appeared.

"Too bad it's not a monster." Nova sounded disappointed.

"It's all good. Let's open it," Chimney added eagerly.

"Wait!" shouted Nova.

Ignoring Nova's plea, Chimney opened the treasure box. There was a flash of light—an explosion—and Chimney's health meter glowed red; he was nearly dead.

What the hell was that?!

"Geez, another bomb," said Chimney.

"You idiot, you could've killed BlackRose! What would you have done if she'd been caught in the blast?"

"Oh yeah. Sorry."

Nova huffed. He chanted a spell and Chimney's hit points returned to normal.

"Are bombs common?" I asked.

"Yeah, but Chimney's also a completist on springing traps."

"A 'completist?' "

"Right. He says he wants to try to spring every kind of trap at least once." Nova turned to his friend. "Don't be like that, Chimney. It's very annoying," he teased.

"Chimney almost died because of a trap?" I gulped. *Were these guys totally nuts?*

"Blue treasure boxes have traps planted in them. You just gotta use a fortune wire and turn them yellow."

"Yellow?"

"Uh-huh. Yellow ones are normal treasure boxes, so if you open them you get items or gold." Nova shrugged.

"I almost always get near-death experiences!" Chimney cried.

Springing traps with no regard to safety didn't seem like fun to me! *Whatever floats your boat . . . I guess The World has something for all types.*

For the next hour they taught me the basics of combat, until I told them I had to get some sleep. I logged off, feeling grateful for the lesson.

If I wanted to support Kite, I'd have to get better at battle. I also needed to grow stronger. I couldn't stand relying on others to protect me.

●◆●

Over the next few days, I visited various fields: scorched landscapes, frozen wastelands, nighttime wildernesses, and dense forests where it was easy to become lost.

I invoked magic portals and found treasure and monsters. Once, I got surrounded by too many enemies . . . and BlackRose died for the first time.

It was extremely unpleasant. Afterward, I played more cautiously.

Once my character reached Level 13, I e-mailed Kite:

```
I read a message on the BBS that
mentioned the girl and that black
thing you were talking about. Do you
want to look for them on the Theta
server?
```

• ◆ •

Dun Loireag was the root town on the Theta server. Built on a small plain that was surrounded by towering, rocky mountains, it had a Scottish Highlander theme. The shops and houses were built into sheer rock cliffs. Bridges linked many of the areas together . . . though calling them "bridges" was more than I thought they deserved, since they were just sloping wooden planks (with no railings) leading from one platform to another.

The sound of the wind rushed constantly in my ears. Even though I knew it was only a game, as an acrophobe, the thought of crossing the bridges terrified me. In spite of my fear, I looked down, trying to find the base of the mountain. Bad idea. All I could see were clouds below me. I scurried away from the edge.

Compared to Mac•Anu, this place was much smaller, more like a village. I explored the area while I waited for Kite.

One lot I came across had a sign out front with a picture of a pig on it. But the bizarre-looking animals I could see in the back of the lot didn't resemble anything in real life, least of all pigs. I looked at the sign once more. *Is this some kind of ranch?*

I decided to talk to the computer-generated character that ran the place. I guess gaming lingo referred to them as NPCs, for Non-Player Characters.

He explained that he raised and sold the small creatures penned up in the back. They were called grunties.

Grunties? What the hell kind of name is that?

I continued through the town for a little while before getting bored and then just returning to the Chaos Gate to wait for Kite. I'm not exactly a patient person.

Finally, he showed.

"You know it's impolite to keep a girl waiting!" I joked.

"Sorry about that." He shrugged.

"We're going to Quiet, Eternal, White Devil, right?"

"Yeah."

"Okay! Let's go!" I said, joining his party.

"Is it okay if I invite someone else along?" he asked.

"Huh?!" This was unexpected.

"He's a Heavy Axeman. He'll be good to have along."

"I guess I don't mind. What kind of person is he?"

"Hmm. Well, rather than me trying to explain him, why don't you just see for yourself? I'm sure he'll be along any moment."

"Fine," I answered curtly. *Am I the only one who doesn't want to involve unrelated people?* The beginnings of dread pricked my heart.

"You know what?" Kite spoke suddenly.

"What?"

"I did some searching without you."

"You did?" I was surprised.

"Yeah. Sorry. But we just met the other day."

"Yeah, I know."

"Well, I wanted to follow a few leads on my own," he said.

"What did you find out?" I asked.

"I read on the boards about this place that looked like a dried-up ocean."

"Yeah, I was just there, too."

"You were?" Something in his voice sounded strained.

"Yes."

"Oh." He stared at me.

"See, you should have taken me along!" I teased.

"Well, when did you go?"

"Just the other night," I answered.

"But you're okay, right?" He sounded worried.

"Yeah, why?" I asked.

"Did you meet anything like we did before?"

"No. Did you?" Before he answered, I knew that he had. "Tell me what happened," I demanded.

He sighed and told me that he'd visited the field a few days earlier, before I went with Nova and Chimney. Unlike when we'd gone, there had been an NPC standing guard at the entrance to the dungeon. He warned Kite to return to town, but Kite ignored him and continued forward.

When Kite arrived at the deepest point of the dungeon, he encountered a cheerfully reckless Wavemaster and together they fought a Data Bug.

I realized that if I had taken Chimney and Nova there first, we might have been in danger. I had the feeling that there was some connection between the Data Bugs and the places where the girl had been sighted.

Next, Kite told me about Piros, the Heavy Axeman for whom we were waiting. Kite had met Piros in a dungeon where an ogre was giving him the spanking of a lifetime, immediately after Piros had bragged about what a kick-ass fighter he was.

"I couldn't sit back and let him die, so I ended up lending him a hand," Kite said with a smile.

I tried not to laugh. "Hey, does this Piros guy know about the virus?"

"No."

"Well then are you sure you want to involve him in this?!" I asked, incredulous.

"I don't *want* to, but I need companions." Kite rubbed his right arm where he wore the bracelet that the girl had given him.

Then it hit me. *Kite can fight Data Bugs with the power of the bracelet.* I, on the other hand, was utterly powerless against the irregular monsters. Even though we shared the same goal, Kite was far more powerful than me.

"Hey," Kite asked, suddenly very serious, "do you know about protected areas?"

After listening to Yuuji talk so often about message board rumors, I'd made it a habit to check the BBS diligently. Some of the threads had mentioned the protected areas.

"Those are places that can't be accessed from a Chaos Gate," I said. "If you try to enter, you show up, see a warning indicator, and then you're warped back to town."

"Yeah, but I went to a protected—"

Our conversation was interrupted as a huge green mass abruptly appeared before us. "You've done well summoning me! Now let us begin our harrowing journey!"

Say what?

"You there, woman! I am honored to make your acquaintance. I am the Lone Wolf, Piros the Silver White!"

"Uh, hi. I'm BlackRose." I keyed the motion for a bow, but he didn't notice.

"Let us begin our quest!"

I clicked into Whisper Mode so I could speak to Kite without Piros hearing. "Can you finish telling me your story?" I pressed.

"You'll understand soon enough."

Perhaps Kite was taking us to a protected area now. *Is that possible?*

We warped to the field.

"We got right in." Kite sounded surprised, as if we shouldn't have been able to get there that easily.

The scenery of this place was very different from any of the other fields I had visited.

Purple clouds hung low in the sky; snowflakes danced through the air. What at first appeared to be a line of trees in the distance was actually a rip in the very fabric of the game.

The trees were actually green glyphs; symbols and letters that looked like programming language. The characters zigged and zagged like snakes across a black void. Even the snow-covered ground sported occasional fissures that revealed the computer code.

"Well now, this is rather strange, isn't it?"

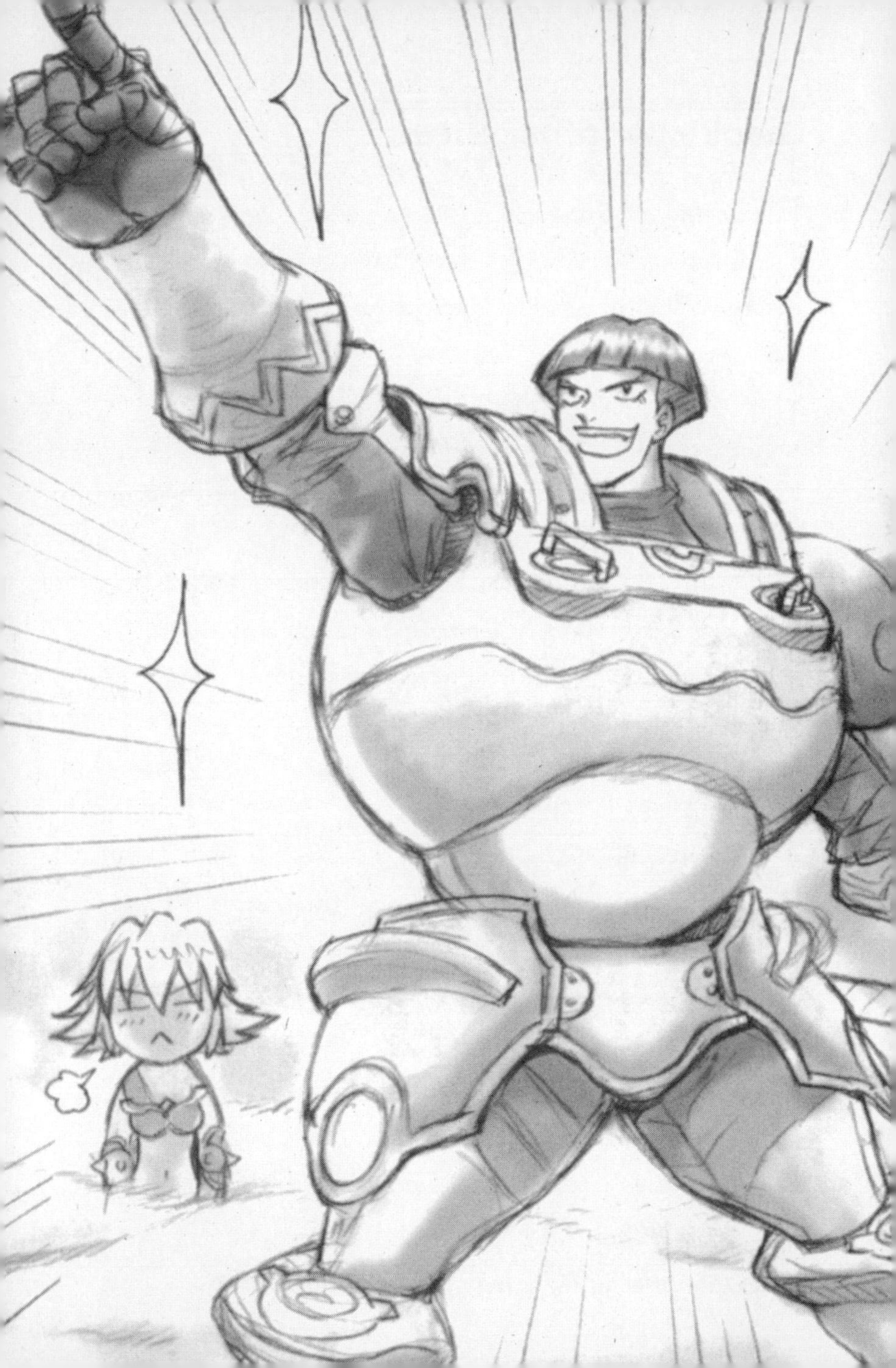

I could tell Piros was as bewildered as I was.

Occasionally, a scream rent the silence, and when it did, the color of the scene inverted. *Isn't that the sign of a Data Bug?*

"It's the same as the other day," Kite muttered as he looked around.

"What do you mean?" I asked. "Hidden, Forbidden, Holy Ground on Delta didn't look this bad."

"No, not there. This is what it was like in Expansive, Haunted, Sea of Sand on Delta when I went there."

"Well, let's proceed!" Piros said grandly. "Standing around avails us nothing, boys!"

"I'm a girl!"

"Oh, yes! Girls, then!"

"But Kite's not a girl!" I said.

Kite watched our exchange and laughed. I felt my tension ease, but only a little.

We entered the dungeon.

It was the same as the field. The floors and walls contained rips revealing the same lines of meaningless alphanumeric characters.

"Wasn't entry to this field prohibited?" Piros asked.

A Bolt from the Blue

"But we got in," Kite said, confused.

"Hmm. Of course! Then the prohibition was lifted, but the reason for this is shrouded in the reek of secrecy!" Piros concluded. "I see! Then we have come to expose the terrible secret, right, boys?!"

"I told you, we aren't all *boys!*"

"I apologize, BlackRoast."

"As long as you remember this time . . . Wait, what? 'Roast?!' Get my name right!"

Piros annoyed me to no end. I just prayed he was trying to be funny.

We continued forward, my heart skipping a beat every time we turned a bend in the passage or descended a staircase. The farther we went, the more my fear of Data Bugs was overshadowed by my hope that we might encounter the girl who had granted Kite his power. At least she could explain what it was and why it worked. *Perhaps if we understood that, we might understand the reason Kite's friend and Fumikazu are in comas.*

We were descending a staircase when Kite suddenly stopped.

"It's a dead end," he announced.

That was very odd.

"Well! We have mastered this dungeon," Piros said grandiosely. "There was no mystery. Now, friends, let us return to town!"

But the fact that there was no mystery was itself a mystery. We'd explored every room and passageway, yet we hadn't encountered anything at all.

"They're not here." Kite's voice echoed hollowly through the dim darkness of the dead-end passage. "Neither the black creature nor the girl."

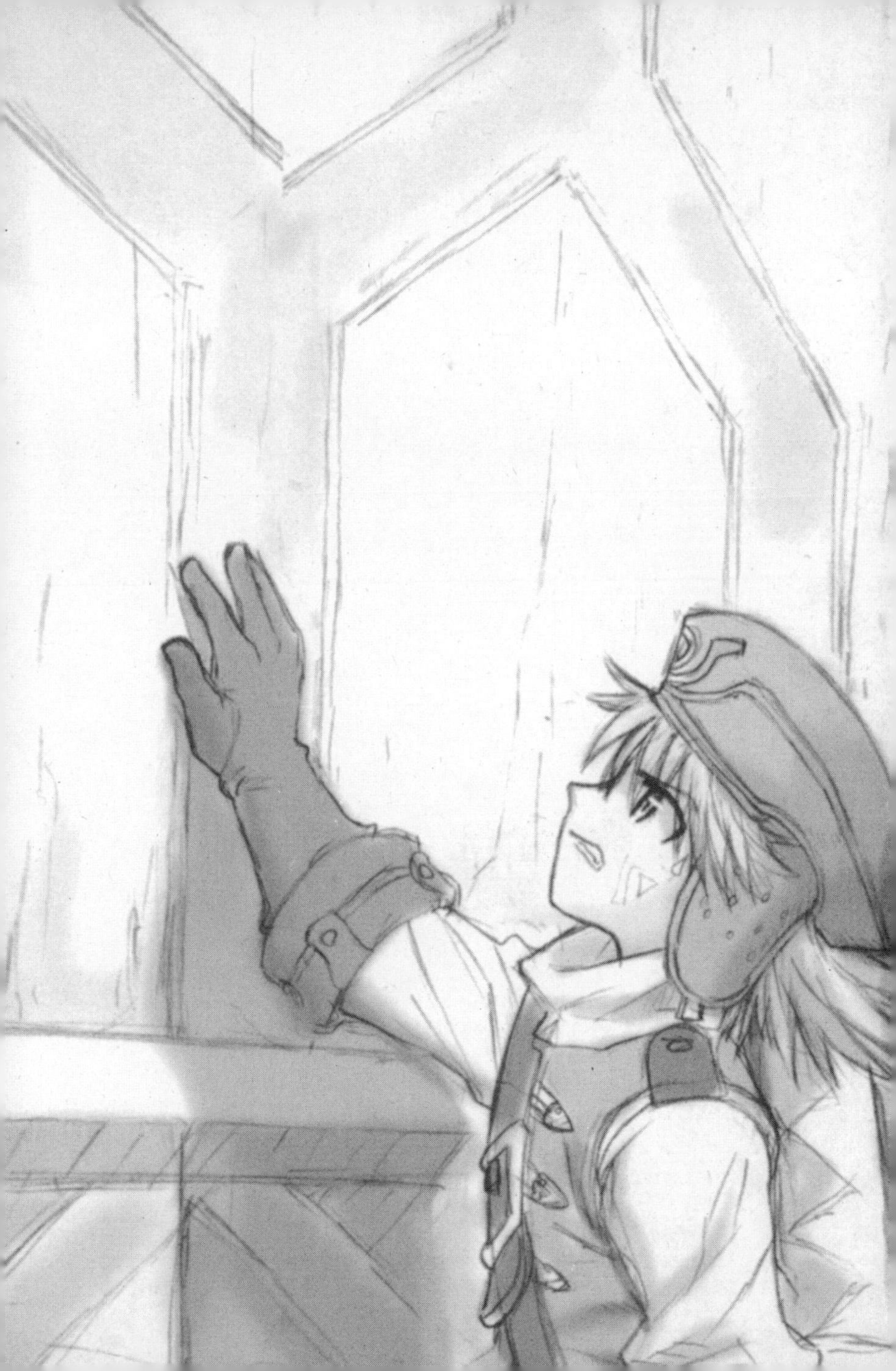

Bullying and the White Room

I decided to write an e-mail to Marin, the person who'd first posted the thread about the mystery girl on the BBS. Assuming the post hadn't been a complete fabrication in the first place, something must have happened after it was posted. If the information was intentionally false—which was entirely possible—I didn't think she would answer, but I had a feeling I could get at least some kind of reaction. All I could do was wait.

I arrived early at Dun Loireag for my rendezvous with Kite and wandered around. Finding myself back at the grunty ranch, I checked out the strange animals to kill some time. Somehow, while lost in thought, I agreed to buy one of the disgusting little creatures from the NPC rancher.

I tried canceling, but it didn't work. The rancher just smiled at me and kept repeating, "You made a good choice. The grunty is a fun companion."

My grunty was the size of a puppy, with a pig-shaped body and a squashed face. It looked up at me with watery eyes.

"Mama, fooood," whined the grunty.

Is it speaking to me? I didn't know these things could talk!

Its eyes shined in anticipation, its tail frantically wagging as it looked at me. I already had my hands full taking care of Fumikazu's prairie dog, Hana. *Could I handle taking care of a pet in real life and in the game?*

I asked the rancher how to care for it. He explained that I had to feed it regularly and that it eventually would grow to its "third stage," whatever that meant, and then it would be large enough for me to ride in the fields. It seemed hard to believe that this tiny creature could grow to the size of a horse.

Maybe I'll grow attached to the grunty as I grew attached to Hana?

"I'm telling you now, I'm very busy," I warned the grunty, but it simply wagged its tail.

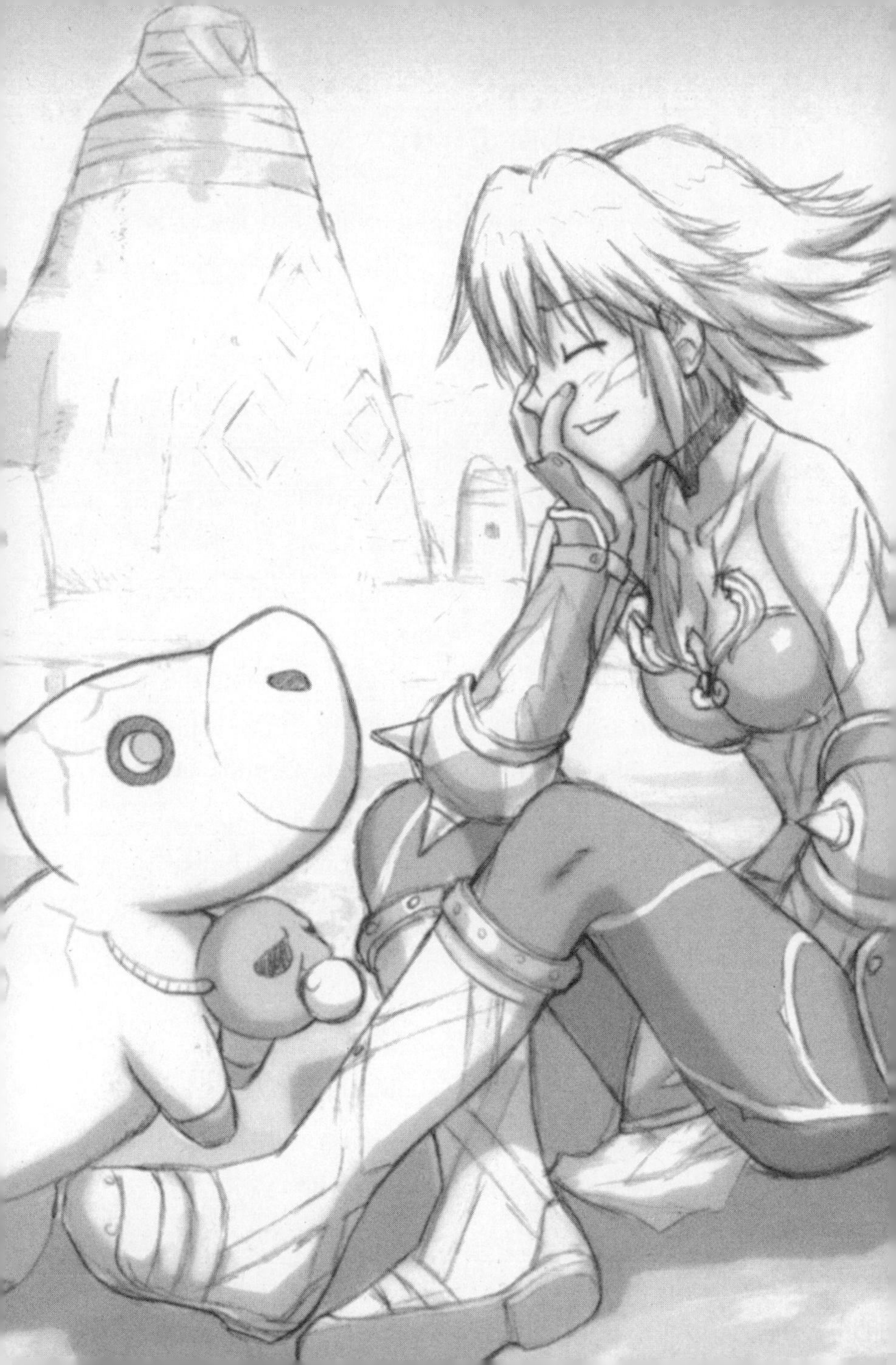

I returned to the rendezvous point and found Kite waiting.

"Been here long?" I asked.

"Nope," Kite replied. Then I noticed another character waiting with him—a fidgety Twin Blade in blue clothes. Her outfit showed off her short emerald hair. The arms and legs of her slender body were painted with unique designs.

"Um . . . who are you?" I asked. *Has he roped another innocent bystander into this mess?*

She looked at Kite and beamed.

"This is someone I helped the other day when she had trouble getting to a Gott Statue," said Kite. "I just happened to meet her again near the Chaos Gate here. I thought we'd play as a party of three today."

"I'm Natsume! It's nice to meet you!" She bowed and smiled awkwardly. For some reason, I felt like I should keep my eye on her.

"I'm BlackRose. Likewise!" I replied.

They invited me into their party.

Will we be all right with this new girl tagging along? I guess Kite considers her another companion. I wondered what his criteria were for inviting people along on perilous journeys, but then I had to admit I'd done almost the same thing with Nova and Chimney.

"Wow, BlackRose! You're a Heavy Blade. Cool!" Natsume said in a shrill voice as she ogled the large sword on my back.

"Uh . . . yeah?"

"I'll do my best to be a reliable resource for the party, too!" she said.

"I'm not very reliable myself," I muttered.

"Huh? Kite was just saying how reassuring it is to be with you!"

"He was?" I said, surprised. *He was being too courteous. I hadn't been reliable to him at all.*

A blue-haired Wavemaster walked up to Kite. "Do you have a minute?" he asked.

Is this another one of Kite's acquaintances?

"Sure. Why aren't you with Mia today?" Kite wondered aloud.

The boy looked embarrassed and started fidgeting.

"Is something wrong with Mia, Elk?" Kite asked.

Elk lifted his head and said no more. I realized that they had switched to private chat.

Natsume and I stood around like idiots, waiting for them to finish. I was about ready to put the FMD down and go make some tea when Kite finally broke the silence.

"Sorry. I can't go anywhere with you today," he said, shaking his head. "Elk needs me with him—it's very important. I'll contact you later!"

"What?!" Natsume cried, flustered.

"I'm really sorry! I'll e-mail you later!"

Kite quickly ran toward the Chaos Gate with Elk and they disappeared, leaving me alone with Natsume.

"I can't believe he left like that," Natsume whined like an abandoned puppy.

"How can he do that?" I was more angry than annoyed. *How can he leave me with a girl I've only just met?!*

I could have ditched Natsume, but I figured I should be courteous. "What are your plans, Natsume? I was thinking of jumping into a field solo."

She turned, startled.

"Do you want to go together?" I asked, inviting her into a party. I couldn't just leave her here.

"Yes! I'll do my best!" she replied joyously.

"What places have you visited so far?" I asked.

Bullying and the White Room

"I've often gone to a place called bursting-something. It was written on the BBS as being newbie-friendly."

"Bursting?"

"Yeah, that was the A coordinate."

Remembering how I randomly chose coordinates for Fumikazu brought up bitter memories. *I need to take Natsume someplace safe!*

"I don't really care where we go," she continued. "Why don't you choose?"

"Oh. Okay."

We went to the Chaos Gate. It was my first time as a party leader. I'd have to choose carefully. I couldn't afford to make any mistakes.

I scanned through the menus.

"Let me see here . . ." I said, as I threw some words together. "Buried, Orange, Gate . . . ?"

How about that?

It was Level 25. *Impossible.* I was only Level 20 and Natsume a mere 13. Anything beyond Level 16–18 would be too hard.

I thought Beautiful, Her, Scent had a nice ring to it. But it was Level 22.

There sure were a lot of high-level fields on the Theta server. I wondered if any would be suited to Natsume.

"Find anything yet?" Natsume asked hopefully.

"Not yet. Let me keep looking."

Sinking, Someone's, Scaffold came up next. I didn't like those words. They felt ominous. But the area level was only 17.

"Is that no good?" Natsume inquired.

"Um . . . I guess it'll have to do."

Natsume and I warped to a surprisingly beautiful scene: gently falling snowflakes descended from a beautiful winter sky.

I could see other characters wandering around, so I thought it would be safe. The key warning sign would be broken scenery revealing computer code. I didn't see any.

As we walked, Natsume told me how she'd met Kite.

She had entered a dungeon hoping to acquire some new equipment, but her level wasn't high enough and she had to flee to keep from getting killed. When she returned to the entrance, she encountered Kite. Once she explained her situation, Kite kindly offered to help her find a new magic item.

Bullying and the White Room

Natsume proudly showed off what she had found. "These Twin Blades are my key treasure—they're Spiral Edge!"

Kite could be really nice, even to total strangers. He reminds me a little of my brother.

"I want to become strong like Kite! I've got to try hard!" Natsume declared as she tightly grasped her Spiral Edge.

Kite's strength wasn't just in his character's level—it was in his personality. But she was right; I had to be strong, too.

Once Natsume had had enough of the fighting (and treasure hunting) in that area, we returned to town and I logged off for the day.

She was nicer than I first thought possible. I e-mailed Kite my thoughts and told him we'd had fun adventuring, but that I hoped we could get back to our shared goal soon.

● ⬡ ●

"Bye! See you tomorrow!" As I hurried to tennis practice, I waved to friends who were leaving for the day. I was running late, so I took the stairs to the lockers two at a time. When I arrived at the door, I could hear voices inside.

"I hate when people shirk their responsibilities!"

"I can't believe she was chosen when she can't even get here on time."

"Maybe they'll replace her before the season is over."

Are they referring to me? I opened the door and the room fell silent. I walked past the cold stares and quickly changed.

It had been my turn for classroom cleanup and hall duty, so I'd told Captain Koura earlier that I'd be late. I was actually on time for tennis practice; I just didn't have time to help with setup.

When I arrived at the court, I apologized to Koura for being late.

"What do you mean? You're right on time."

"Yeah, but I couldn't help with setup today."

"That's all right. I found someone to cover when you told me earlier. It's no big deal," she said, smiling. "Let's have another good day out here today!"

"Akira, you're early!" Risa said half-jokingly. "Did you switch with someone for hall duty or something?"

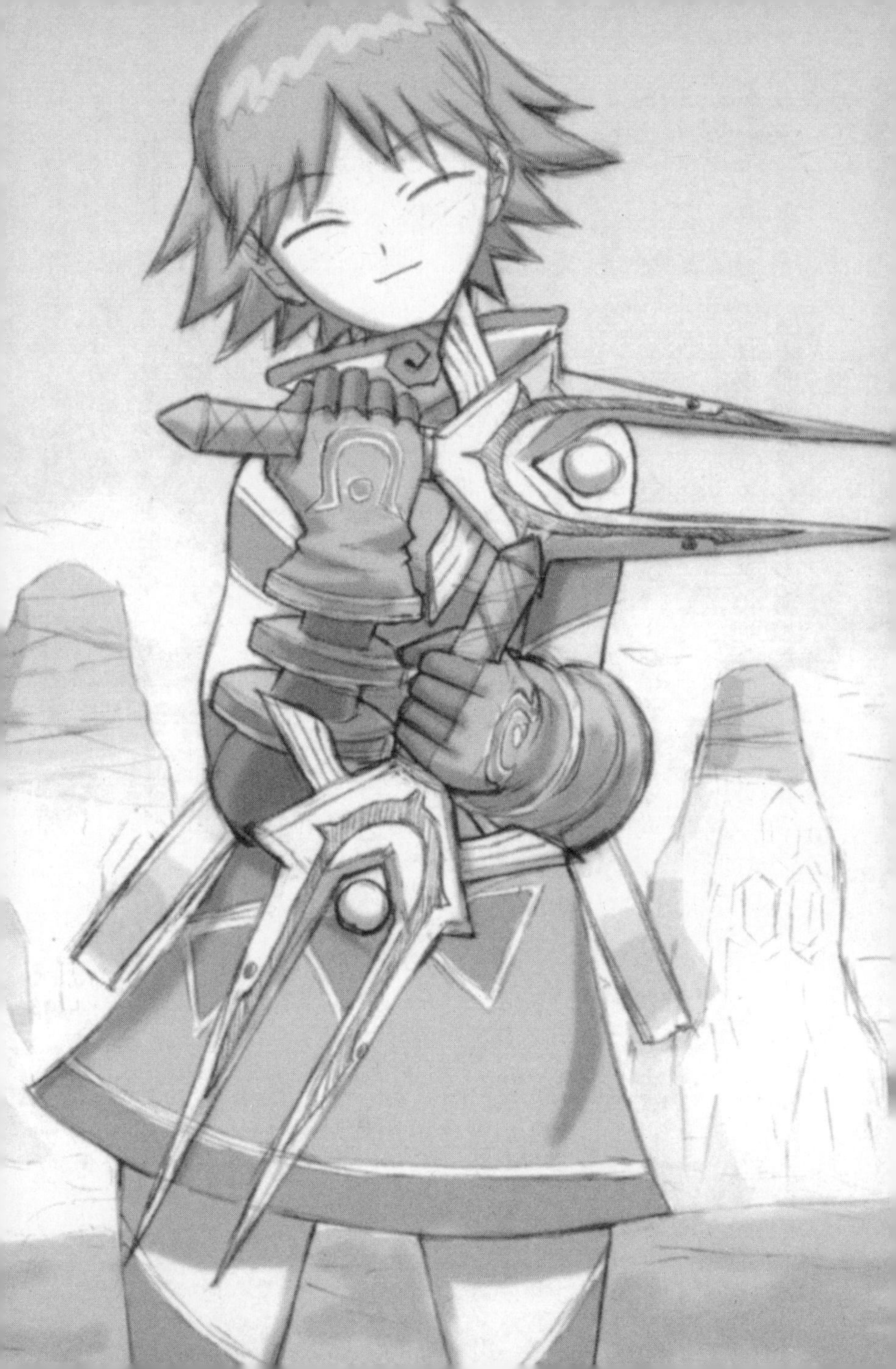

"Not a chance," I replied. "I just finished and rushed over here as soon as I could." As Risa and I talked, I watched the other freshmen getting ready. Normally, they would joke with each other, but today everyone silently concentrated on their tasks. Maybe it was my imagination, but something was off today.

During practice, I felt everyone's eyes on me. But whenever I turned around, everyone quickly looked away. I couldn't understand what had changed since the previous day.

After practice ended, I grabbed hold of the net to help clean up.

"Aren't you tired, Hayami? We'll take care of cleanup," said a freshman who had never spoken to me before. Though she acted polite, I could tell she just wanted me to leave.

"It's okay!" I reassured her. "It's faster when everyone helps out."

I certainly was tired, but I didn't want to complain about it. Cleanup was done by freshmen; that's the way things were. I was a freshman; it didn't matter that I was first string and they weren't.

Bullying and the White Room

As I walked to the storeroom to put away the net and balls, I noticed Risa wasn't around. Usually, she would wait for me so we could walk home together.

"Where's Risa?" I asked the girl who'd spoken to me earlier.

"Got me," she replied curtly.

Is Risa avoiding me, too?!

I rushed back to the locker room, where some of the upperclassmen were still chattering away. Risa wasn't there either, and her bag wasn't in the locker we shared.

If she had to leave early, why didn't she say anything to me during practice?

"Good practice today!" I said to the upperclassmen. No one responded. I shrugged; perhaps they were too engrossed in their own conversations to hear me.

I quickly changed and left.

On days I had practice, I rode my bike to school—I only rode the bus on the other days, when I would visit the hospital. As I kneeled down to unlock my bike, I heard a voice shout, "Hey, wait up!"

It's Risa! "Where were you?" I asked.

"I had to meet Asaoka. Didn't anyone tell you?"

"No." I shook my head.

"I asked them to tell you to wait for me."

"You did?"

"Of course." She frowned.

"No one said anything to me."

"Oh well, I'm sure they were just tired and forgot." She laughed off the incident, but I could tell that my problems were probably just beginning.

● ⬡ ◆

When I opened my locker the following day, my heart nearly jumped out of my chest. Someone had maliciously cut the laces on my shoes. It was a clear cut, like someone took scissors right up the center.

Whoever did it didn't stick around to see my reaction. I was alone. I had some spares, so I quickly replaced the laces and tried not to let it get to me. But it was a struggle. I didn't understand why this was happening. *Did I do something to make someone angry with me? But, what?*

Once I'd calmed down, I noticed Risa's stuff was gone. I went to look for her outside.

Bullying and the White Room

Risa had always been my workout partner, but today she was paired off with an upperclassman. I tried to get her attention, but she didn't look my way. I couldn't just stand there, so I exercised by myself. A few minutes after I started, Koura ran up to me.

"Hayami, you can't do warm-ups alone. Why didn't you say something?" Before I could make an excuse, she called Asaoka over. "When you're alone, ask Asaoka to help you."

"Hey! I can help you with warm-ups! You ready?" Asaoka said eagerly.

"Thank you," I replied.

During practice, I could feel my teammates' cold stares. I tried to ignore them, but they bored into me.

My rally partner (another girl who didn't get picked) hit so hard that I spent the entire practice chasing balls from one end of the court to the other. She was merciless, and by the time we finished, I was exhausted.

Practice continued like this for the rest of the week. I got used to the hard practices, but I couldn't stand everybody's cold attitude.

Even though it bothered me, I came home each night and acted cheerful, no matter how tired or lonely I felt.

I couldn't bring my school problems to the dinner table; we had enough things to worry about as it was. But I was getting seriously depressed on the inside.

● ◆ ●

I had a reply from Marin. She wrote that someone had actually *rewritten* the coordinates in her original post! She couldn't imagine why or for what reason, but she said she was thoroughly creeped out; she passed along the coordinates she'd originally written, but strongly advised me not to go there.

The fact that some hacker or even an administrator had rewritten her post meant someone was trying to hide something. It only intensified my desire to go.

I wrote to Kite, and we met up on Theta server to go to Cursed, Despaired, Paradise, but when we tried the gate, the location was protected; instead of warping us to the field when we picked the final menu item, a new screen interface popped up with some sort of cross-shape. The cross looked like it was made out of crystals with missing shards. I couldn't tell what we were supposed to do with it.

"Argh!" I said. "Kite, didn't you mention something before about getting into protected areas?"

"Gate-hacking isn't that easy," he replied. "To break the protection I need to gather more Virus Cores—which I can only get by using Data Drain on monsters or Data Bugs."

I didn't know how he'd learned to gate-hack, but I imagined the ability came from the same source as his bracelet. Though I felt near my breaking point, I did the only thing I could. I waited.

• ⬡ •

When practice ended, the juniors quickly returned to the locker room. So did the freshmen. After all, they had asked so nicely if I could clean up alone today. How could I refuse?

I hoped that it might make up for whatever I had done to get everyone on my case. *But what could I have done?*

I always greeted everyone when I arrived, I always helped out wherever I could, and I always played my best.

Even though playing the "victim" was never a very attractive role, I couldn't help feeling sorry for myself. I had the tears to prove it, too. I hated crying, but I couldn't help it.

"Akira!" Risa called to me as I carried the net back to the storeroom. I quickly wiped the tears from my eyes.

"Someone just told me you were cleaning up by yourself."

"Yeah, it's fine. I guess the others had something else to do."

Without another word, Risa jumped in to help. After a while, she asked, "Akira, are you okay?"

I could tell she was worried. At the same time, I couldn't believe she was acting like she didn't know what was going on. She must have noticed how strangely people were treating me. Even she seemed to avoid me at times, and she knows my brother is in the hospital. *Of course I'm not okay!*

"Yeah, I'm fine," I lied.

Risa gulped. "Akira, I'm sorry."

I didn't want to hear it. "All done! Let's hurry up and change so we can go home."

The lights were still on in the locker room. The upperclassmen's voices were barely audible:

"I can't stand Hayami's attitude."

Bullying and the White Room

"Stupid freshmen don't know anything."

"It's like nothing can touch her as long as Koura's got her back!"

"She doesn't complain, but it's just an act."

"How about we go after Asaoka next?"

"Sure, that sounds fun. As long as Koura doesn't notice."

I couldn't believe they were bullying me just for being picked in the singles division! I felt dizzy.

Get a grip! You haven't done anything wrong!

Ever since Fumikazu had collapsed, I'd decided I wouldn't complain about anything. I entered the locker room as calmly as I could.

"Good practice today!"

They stopped talking the instant I spoke. I concentrated on walking toward my locker. My legs shook.

Risa's equipment was still missing from the locker. *When will things return to normal? Or will it be like this from now on?*

"Hayami's here; want to leave?" I heard a girl say from the other side of some lockers. I stiffened.

"Yeah, let's get outta here."

I quickly changed and walked toward my bike.

Even though I now knew why I was being picked on, there was nothing I could do about it. As a gym teacher, my dad must have seen this sort of thing all the time.

I remembered something he once told me: "Even if you're bullied, play fair."

I was. But it bothered me a great deal. I was getting completely ostracized. Who *wouldn't* be bothered?

Dad also told me to talk about it with someone I could trust.

Who could I trust? Captain Koura? Asaoka? I couldn't tell them. That would seem like tattling. I didn't want to do something so lame, and I sure didn't want to make it worse than it already was.

I understood how the upperclassmen who hadn't gotten picked must feel. But I wasn't responsible. If they had something to say to me, they should just say it to my face.

I wondered if I could handle the responsibility of being on the tennis team *and* discovering the cause of Fumikazu's coma. Maybe it was impossible to do both. Lately, my world felt as if it were about to crumble.

"Pull yourself together! Don't wimp out!" I told myself while riding down the street.

Bullying and the White Room

I could be strong. I could still fight. I could be BlackRose. I didn't have to let their taunts get to me. After all, I still had friends.

I came home exhausted, but I still needed to go online. Fortunately, it was the weekend, so I could sleep in. I booted up my PC.

I had an e-mail from Kite with yesterday's date on it. He'd finally gotten his hands on a Virus Core, and we could now enter the protected area. I had a bad feeling . . .

● ⬡ ●

I had to forget my schoolmates' jealousy and focus on the game. At least in The World, I was strong.

I met up with Kite at the Theta server Chaos Gate. "Hi. You ready to go to Cursed, Despaired, Paradise?"

"Sure. Do you mind if someone comes along?" Kite replied.

"Who?" I asked, wary.

"A Wavemaster I helped out the other day."

"Uh, that's fine, but why didn't you mention anything before now?"

"I didn't think it would be a big deal. Is it?"

Kite had his bracelet, so I guessed we'd be all right. "Nah, no problem." I smiled reassuringly, but I worried about the constant string of strangers he brought along.

"Nya ha ha! Sorry for the wait!"

I turned and saw our Wavemaster draped in blue and white baggy clothes. Her pink hair was covered by a hat that was split in two. It hung down like a floppy-eared rabbit. I couldn't believe this was the Wavemaster Kite had talked about. I felt my strength drain.

"Good evening. I'm BlackRose," I said half-heartedly.

"Whatever works, girl. I'm Mistralllll!" She held the "l" much longer than necessary, and her voice seemed too cheerful.

For some reason, it reminded me of the tennis team girls who hated me. *Fake.* Saying I was hostile toward her would be an understatement.

"Are you always this pointlessly cheerful?" I asked.

Mistral stared blankly for a moment. "It's best to keep things fun, isn't it? If you think toooo much about stuff, they aren't fun anymore."

"So you don't worry about anything?"

Bullying and the White Room

"Nyaaa ha haa! I sure don't. After all, I've got nothing to worry about."

"Must be nice not to have any hardships." I folded my arms.

"Hardships?" questioned Mistral. "Of course I have hardships. Everyone alive has good days and bad. But everything we experience only serves to enlighten us!"

She seemed blindly optimistic, like the kind of person who would rearrange deckchairs on the *Titanic.*

"BlackRose, are you all right?" Kite asked, worried.

"I'm fine," I said, embarrassed.

"I'm sorry if I'm buggin' you. I didn't mean to!" Mistral peered at my face. "Whaaat's up? Something must have happened. Keep your chin up!"

Mistral patted me on the head. I felt dizzy.

"Y'know what? I might get to see that technique again today," she said.

Technique? Does she mean the Data Drain?

"Let's go, then!" declared Kite.

"How do we get in?" I asked.

"I'll show you." Kite activated the gate menu and selected the coordinates. When the crystal cross-shape

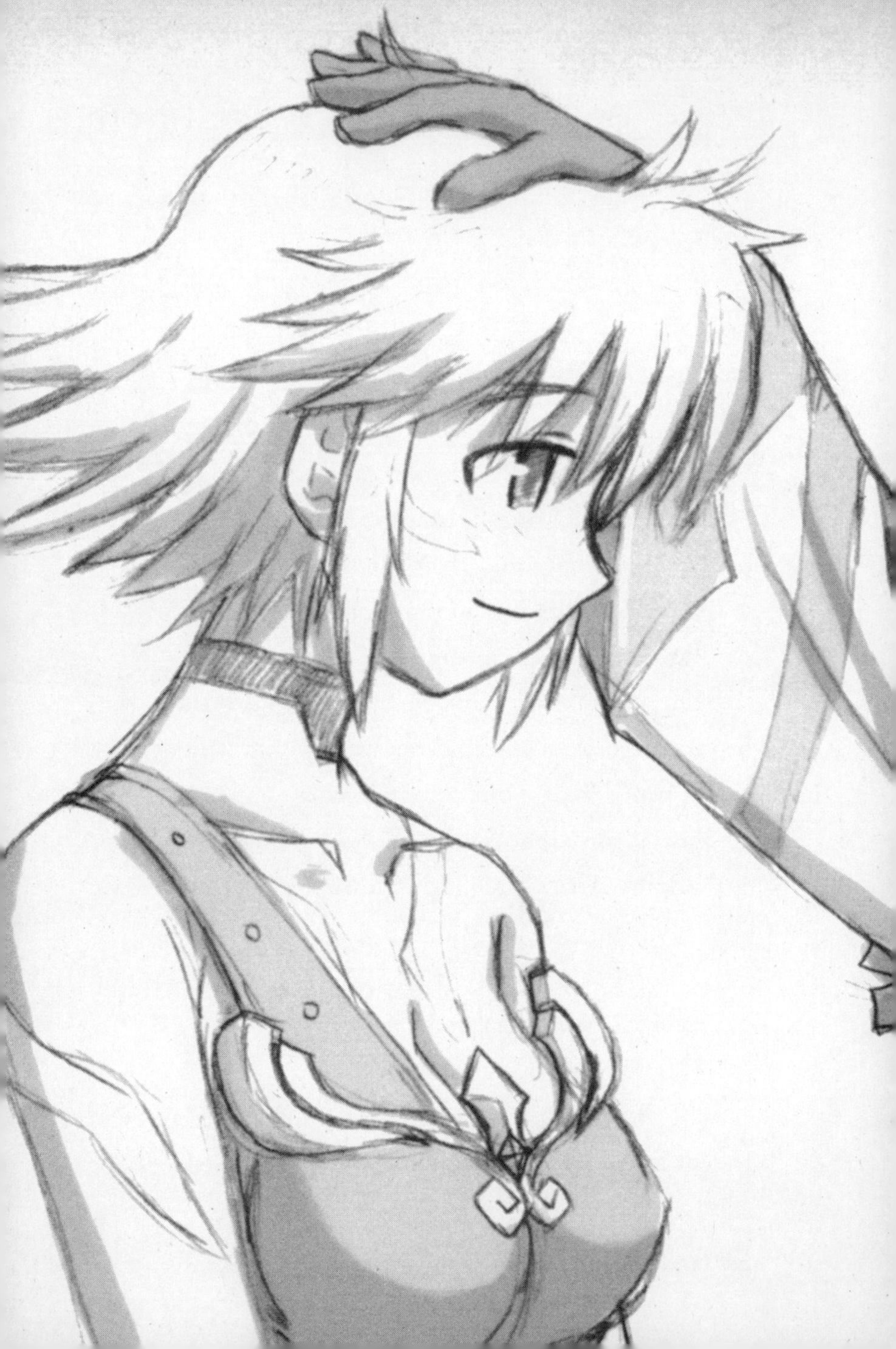

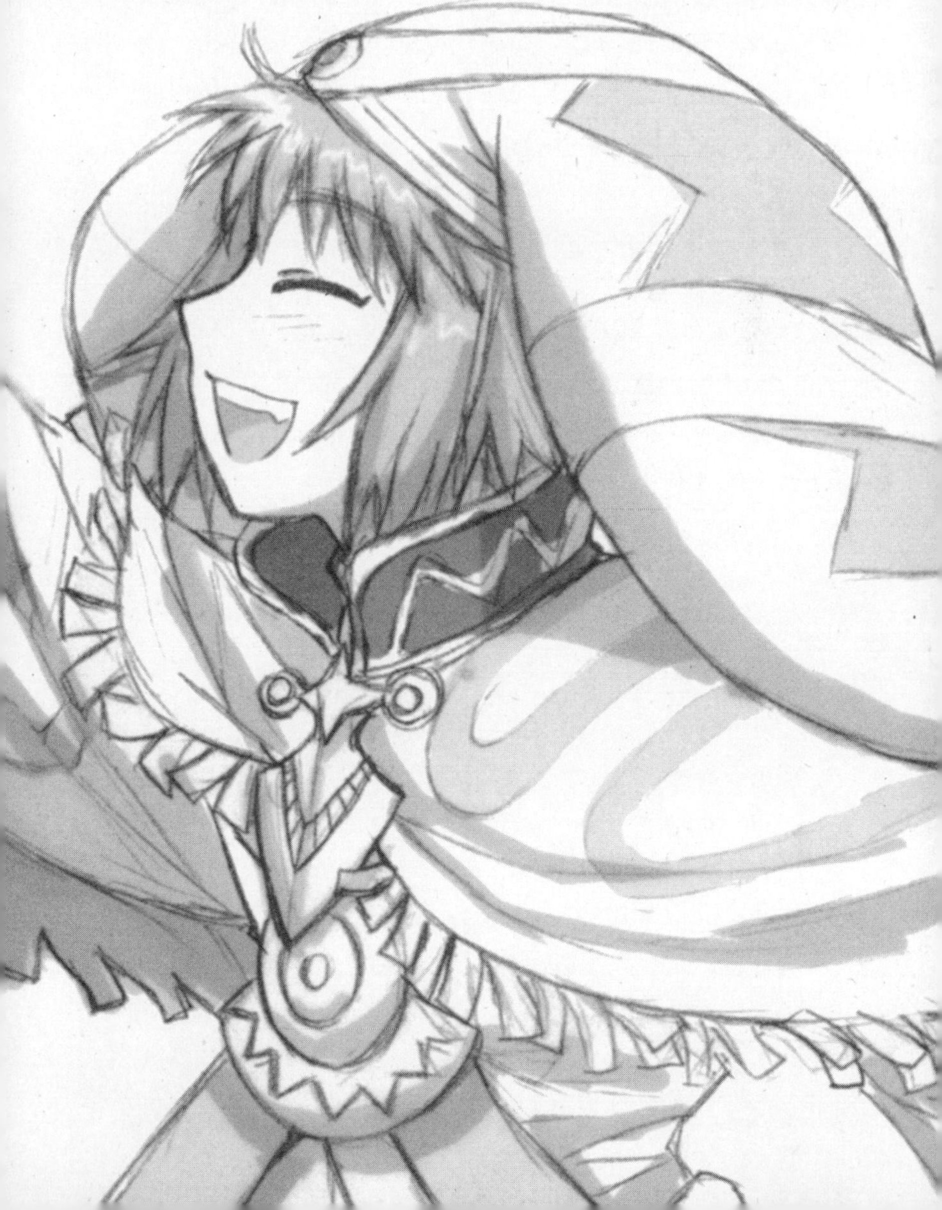

appeared, he produced six shards from his inventory. "These are the Virus Cores," he said. "When I insert them into the right places in these crystals, the protection will be lifted and we'll be able to get in." He got to work.

"Where did you learn to do this?" I asked.

"Mia taught me," he said matter-of-factly.

"Mia?"

"Yeah, didn't he tell you?" Mistral jumped in.

"No," I replied. "Why don't you tell me about Mia?"

"She's someone I met. She looks like a cat." Kite clearly didn't want to talk about it.

"A cat? You mean like a real cat?"

"Noooo!" Mistral cried. "She's like half-cat, half-human."

"Have you met her?" I asked.

"Nope! I only know what he told me," Mistral replied. "But she sounds cool."

A feline figure? I'd never seen anyone like that in The World. And why would she teach Kite how to gate-hack? Better yet, how did she know how to do it?

Clearly, Kite wasn't ready to confide in me, or he would have told me all of this before.

Bullying and the White Room

. ● .

We arrived in another area with broken graphics. The pitch-black ground wriggled as if it were alive. I looked around nervously, expecting to see a Data Bug at any moment.

"Whoa, whoa, whoa!" Mistral looked around. "This is just like the other day."

As we headed for the dungeon, we encountered a giant human hand. Suddenly, Mistral shouted, "Yow! It's moving!"

The dungeon's entrance was actually the mouth of a giant who looked as if he'd been buried alive. We entered his mouth, but it gave me the creeps, like we were being eaten alive. We proceeded cautiously, as monsters hid in every nook and cranny.

"Look, it's the same inside." Kite pointed to the broken graphics within the dungeon.

My heart raced, but I tried to remain focused. *Will we run into a Data Bug?*

We fought our way into the depths, and along the way, Mistral managed to prove useful in combat. She figured out the enemy's weaknesses and quickly exploited them with her magic. At the same time, she kept a close watch on our health and hit us with a recovery spell whenever we were low.

We finally arrived in the deepest part, where a purplish mist obscured a chamber door.

"There it is." I pointed.

"Looks suspicious, and that's promising," Mistral whispered.

"You ready?" Kite asked.

"Yeah. You guys scared?" I asked.

Kite shook his head. Mistral practically jumped into the air. "No, not a bit! Come on, let's go!"

Kite advanced into the fog.

The interior of the room was pure white. There were no discernible boundary lines; everything blended together. Inside the room lay a disturbingly large number of teddy bears.

The bears were scattered everywhere. Their eyes were unfocused, bulging out; their bodies were a dull yellow color. In the center of the room stood a canopy bed. It almost resembled a child's room.

Bullying and the White Room

"Wa-cha-cha, what is this place?" Mistral's voice reverberated around the room.

A man's voice suddenly echoed around us:

"And so I shall name her Aura. Without you, she would not exist—the shining girl, Aura. We will entrust her with our will. Our future is in her hands. She is our—"

"Hey! Is this the ghost everyone's been talking about? Come on out, ghost!" Mistral waved her staff around, but the voice stopped.

I waited nervously to see what would happen. I felt as if the bears were watching us with their hollow eyes.

"What *is* all this?" I asked.

"I don't know, but I wonder if Aura is the girl," said Kite.

"You mean the one who gave you the bracelet?" I asked.

"Yeah." I noticed he touched the bracelet whenever anyone mentioned it.

Something resting on the floor caught my eye. I tried grabbing it, but the moment I touched it, the computer log went crazy, generating the following message:

```
Shunning the field broken by Wave,
The shadowed girl whispers,
"Surely, I will return."
Alas, the truth unbeknownst,
Awaiting her at journey's end;
Eternal mourning for her land.
```

"Are you seeing this?" I asked.

"Yeah," Kite replied.

"What does it mean?" inquired Mistral.

"None of it makes any sense," Kite added.

Is it something from mythology?

We were all bewildered.

Nothing else happened there. The vision of the hollow-eyed teddy bears haunted me for some time afterward.

Looking back on our visit to that strange place, which we later called Harald's Room, I think that must have been the first time we were finally able to step into the hidden kernel of the game. There was a real-world mystery behind the words we heard there. It wasn't just something invented for our amusement.

"The World may be virtual, but those people are real!"

Bullying and the White Room

That's what Fumikazu told me right before he lost consciousness. At that point in time, I thought I understood what he'd meant. Actually, he was saying that, in a sense, The World itself was real.

Yes . . . The World wasn't just some game . . .

Everything Goes Wrong

"What am I supposed to do?" I sighed as I looked at the calendar propped against the side of my PC. Midterms would begin the next day.

I had eight tests over the next three days. The only good news was that tennis practice was suspended during midterms, so I wouldn't have to deal with the catty girls on top of all the cramming.

My textbooks and notes were spread out on my desk, but I couldn't focus on studying. I put on some tea, hoping to change my mood.

As I waited, I wondered what Kite was up to. Maybe there was some new clue posted on the BBS?

Should I check while I'm waiting for the water to boil?

No! I have to concentrate!

Who am I kidding? I already knew I was doomed, so I went online anyway . . .

● ⬢ ●

As could be expected, the first day's exams went terribly.

"Akira, don't look so depressed!" Miho peered into my face as I stared at the ceiling. "The bell's already rung. Come on, let's go home."

Shouko joined us in the hall. "What's wrong, Akira? You think you failed?"

I tried smiling, but they saw through it.

"Don't feel so bad. I'm sure you'll do better tomorrow."

"Yeah, you're good at tomorrow's subjects, aren't you? It's all math and science—the stuff I hate."

I usually did better with formulas and equations than I did in the liberal arts. At least in math you could apply logic and come up with the right answer. *Too bad life isn't like that.*

Shouko patted me on the shoulder as we left school. "Don't let it get to you!"

Everything Goes Wrong

I nodded. In truth, I'd never felt more lonely. How long had it been since I'd last walked home with a friend? For some reason, Risa no longer spoke to me. She ignored me both at practice and in class.

"Akira, is something wrong?" Miho looked worried.

I shook my head.. Something definitely *was* wrong, but I still wasn't going to say anything.

"You shouldn't worry so much. Oh, sorry—I have to run." She pointed to the bus at her stop. "See you tomorrow." Miho waved as she boarded the bus.

That left me and Shouko.

"I have to get going, too," I said as I hopped onto my bike.

"Hey, we've got time, so why not walk?" Shouko asked.

Usually Shouko took the bus as well, so I figured she wanted to hang out—and besides, I could use a friend.

Even though Shouko and I lived near each other, we seldom saw one another outside of school. I knew she lived with her mom, and that they were having trouble making ends meet. Shouko even had to work a part-time job to help out with the family finances. She'd once surprised me at a restaurant when she'd showed up at my table as the waitress.

"It's been forever since I walked home with you, Akira."

I nodded. "We've both been so busy since school started."

We walked in silence, and then Shouko asked the dreaded question . . .

"So, did something happen between you and Risa? Did you two have a fight or something?"

I stopped in my tracks. I didn't know how to answer. "I . . ."

Shouko glanced at me. "What is it?" She looked worried.

"No, nothing's happened," I said, my voice cracking. I forced myself to smile and continued walking.

"You're not hiding anything from me?" she asked.

"No. I'm just worried about Fumikazu. Everything is fine with Risa and me—it's just your imagination." I hated myself for lying, but I didn't want to worry her.

"Okay. If anything does happen, you'll tell me, right?"

"Sure thing."

She sighed. "You always store these things up inside, Akira. Someday you'll get an ulcer."

I probably already have one. "Like I said, there's nothing wrong."

"Yeah, but that was the first time you've mentioned Fumikazu to me in a long time. You're keeping things too bottled up."

She was right.

Shouko and I had a big argument one time in middle school. I don't even remember what we were fighting about, but at one point she yelled something that stuck with me. She said, *"If you think we're friends, tell me anything and everything! If you don't tell me, I can't help you!"*

I wanted to tell her. But there was nothing she could do to help. She couldn't stop the bullying, and she couldn't help Fumikazu. I'd been toughing it out thus far on my own. I didn't see any reason to stop now.

Besides, if I opened up to her, I would crumble. Even *thinking* of the words that sent Fumikazu to the hospital brought tears to my eyes.

When I didn't say anything else, Shouko decided to change the subject.

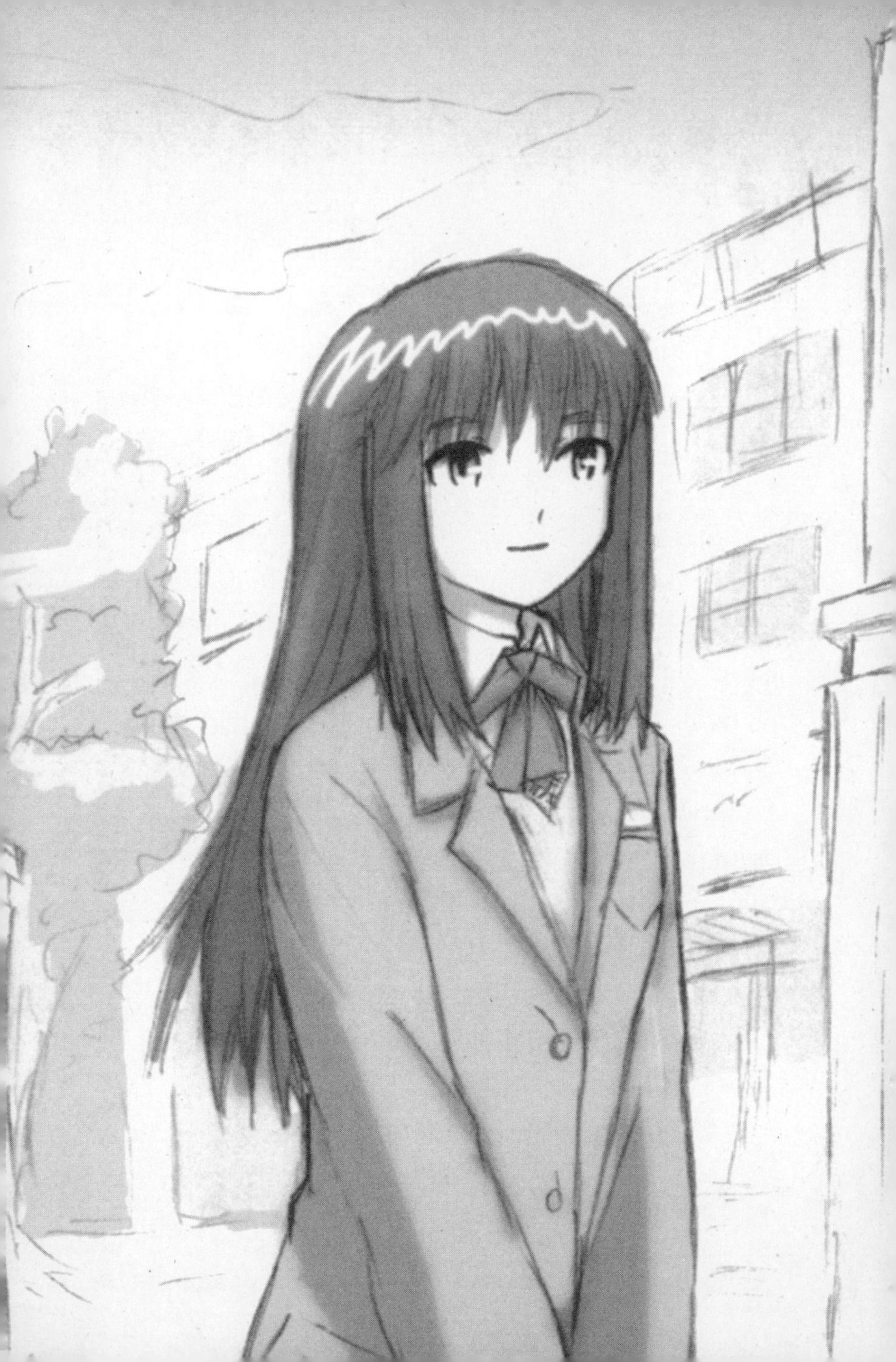

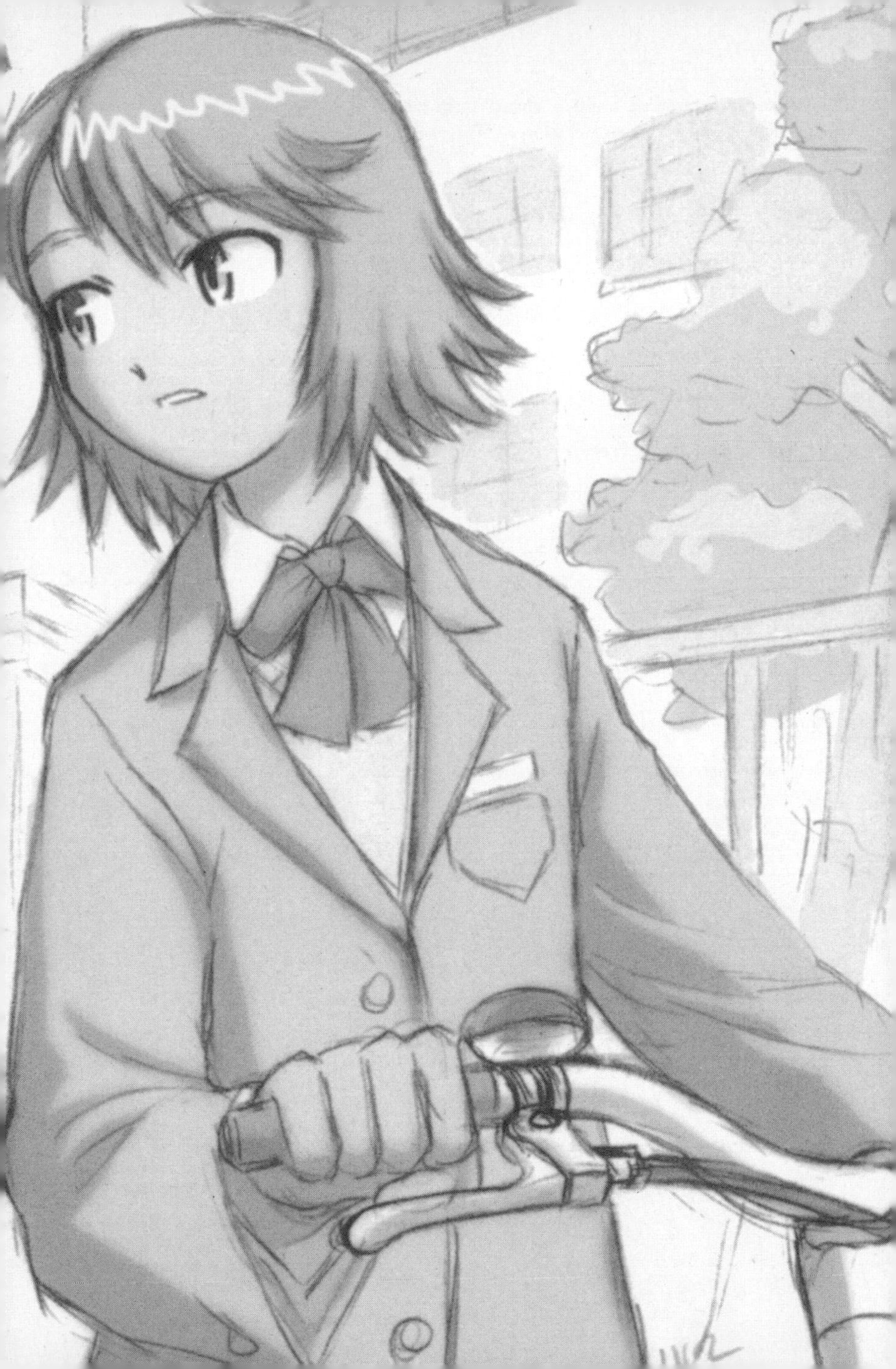

"I know you don't like games, but I have to tell you, it's been weird lately."

She probably meant to switch to a harmless topic, but for me it was like stepping on a land mine. "Do you mean The World?" I asked hesitantly.

"Yeah. It doesn't seem to bother Yuuji, but there are lots of strange rumors going around." Shouko wrinkled her eyebrows, perturbed. "I'm thinking maybe I should quit."

"I think you should!" I spoke too quickly.

Shouko's eyes narrowed suspiciously. "Why do you think that?"

"Uh, well, you say it's bothering you, right?" I answered, trying to smooth over my hasty reply. "If it's just a game, is it really worth getting worked up over?"

"Hmm . . . well, you're right." She laughed. "I shouldn't waste so much time playing games, should I?"

I nodded.

I have to study! My gaze cycled between my textbooks and my computer, then I sighed and sat down in front of the keyboard. *I'll just check the BBS,* I told myself . . . The mail icon blinked. I had a message from Kite.

He'd been investigating a lead and asked if I wanted to meet him.

I wrote back that of course I did.

If I wanted to solve Fumikazu's dilemma, I didn't have a choice. I pushed the textbooks aside.

●◆●

I hadn't been to the Delta server's root town, Mac•Anu, for quite a while. Somehow it seemed busier than before. I looked around until I saw Kite, then called out, "Sorry! Have you been waiting long?"

He looked up and smiled. "Not too long," he said. "Anyway, let's get going. It'll just be the two of us today."

That was fine with me, although I noticed Kite acted differently today; he seemed impatient.

We warped to Buried, Pagan, Fiery Sands and headed directly for the dungeon, as usual. Only this time, we proceeded in silence. It reminded me of the strained quiet that had fallen over my family dinners.

Ugh . . . I'm no good in this kind of atmosphere . . .

The interior of the dungeon resembled the inner workings of a human body—the walls pulsed like they were breathing. I found it unnerving, but Kite moved steadily forward as if he didn't notice.

We entered a room and found a player character waiting for us.

"I'm Linda," she said. "Are you Orca's friend?"

"Yes," Kite answered.

"I heard about that rumor from Bob," she said. "You know, that The World isn't just some 'net game, but that there's something else with an agenda at work."

"What do you think the agenda is?" Kite asked.

"Who knows?" She shrugged. "After all, it's just a rumor. No one knows if it's true or not. But that's what Orca and Balmung were trying to find out, and you know what happened to Orca."

"Balmung?!" I inadvertently shouted.

Balmung was the winged Blademaster I'd met the first day I formed a party with Kite. I thought he was a jerk. But he knew that the monster attacking us was an irregular creature with infinite hit points, and he'd been the one to call it a Data Bug. *Has he been investigating the same thing as us this whole time?*

"Yeah, do you know him?" Linda asked me.

"No, but I met him once."

"Balmung of the Azure Sky, Orca of the Azure Sea . . . the Descendants of Fianna formed the ultimate party," Linda said. "If this could happen to Orca, it could happen to anybody. Take my advice—forget about the rumor."

The Descendants of Fianna. Where have I heard that before?

"I'm afraid I can't do that," Kite replied. "Orca's my friend."

Linda sighed. "I see. In that case, you should go to Lonely, Silent, Great Seal. Orca said he found an odd room there."

"An odd room?!" Kite and I raised our voices at the same time. We looked at each other.

"May the Twilight Dragon's divine protection be with you." Linda gave a mysterious smile and warped out of the dungeon.

"Twilight Dragon? Is that some kind of god?" I asked.

"First I've heard of it, whatever it is," he replied.

"You wanna check out that room?"

"You know it!"

Since it's not possible to warp from one field to another, we stopped back in the root town and warped from there.

Lonely, Silent, Great Seal was a snow field—or it was supposed to be. Again, we found computer code streaming across the landscape.

My spine tingled. I knew we would run into something here.

Kite stood in front of me. I noticed a shadow appear on his back. I stared for a moment as it took shape. It appeared to be a cross.

"Kite," I called, as I looked up to see what cast the shadow.

Kite looked at me strangely, then followed my line of sight to the sky above.

"What is *that?!*" He brought up his Twin Blades.

High above us was a giant human figure, both arms outstretched as it slowly revolved in the sky. Both legs were bound, and its entire body was wrapped in bandages. Four ships flew in circles around it as if they were towing the giant.

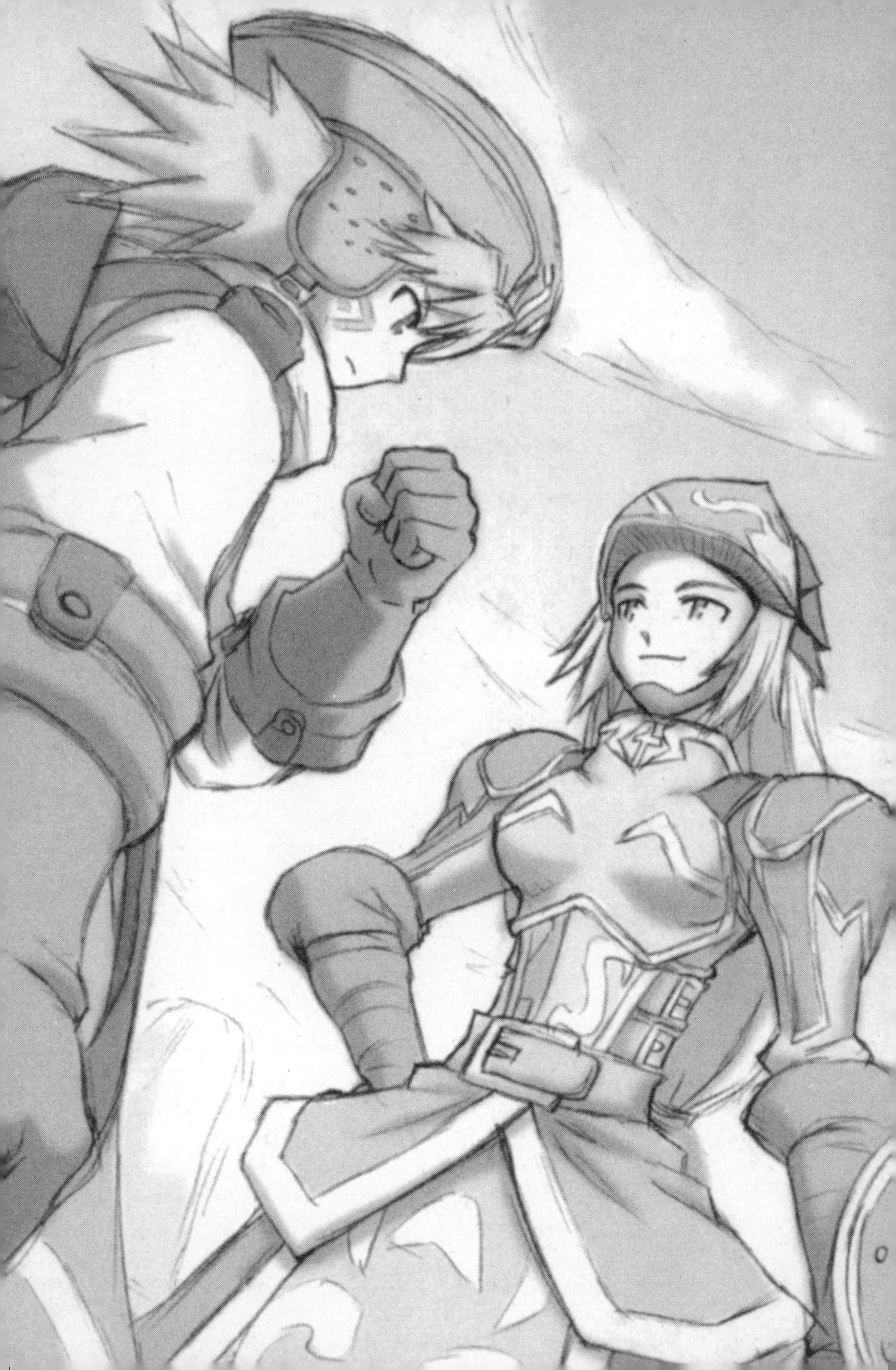

Then the body and ships began to slowly melt into the sky. The outlines blurred until finally they disappeared.

"What do you think that was?" I asked.

"I don't know. It's the first time I've seen it, and I've never heard talk about anything like that."

"Do you think it's an enemy?"

"Maybe." Kite shrugged.

"It was huge! Do you think you could beat something that big?"

"I don't know," Kite answered.

I shouldn't have asked such a dumb question. If we failed to defeat an irregular monster, we'd wind up in a coma. If it came down to a fight, we *had* to win.

"Well, it's gone now. Let's keep moving!" Kite pushed on and we soon discovered the dungeon. The entrance was located in an old stone tower. We lit a torch and entered.

In every respect, the interior resembled an ancient medieval castle. But just like the landscape, its graphics were often broken, and I could see lines of code peeking out at me. No matter how often I saw this, I couldn't get used to it. I feared that something sinister was hiding nearby.

I followed Kite deeper into the dungeon.

When we reached the lowerst point, Kite said, "That's it!" He pointed to the room that Linda had warned us about. A purple mist hung before the entrance.

Kite glanced at me, and then walked forward. Uncertain, I followed.

Just like the other room, a pure white space stretched out before us. But unlike before, there was no canopied bed or weird teddy bears. There was nothing but a void of pure white.

"What kind of room is this?" Kite said. "There's nothing here!"

Then I spied something—a small object on the floor. "Hey, look!" I said, pointing. Kite reached down and picked it up. The event log scrolled by in the window.

"A character string?!"

Instead of an item, it seemed like Kite had picked up just a string of strange characters, almost like a piece of code.

"Can you make any sense of that?" I asked.

Kite shook his head. We tried switching to different fonts and character encodings, but it remained cryptic.

"Well, let's keep looking," I suggested.

We searched the entire space, but it was empty. "It's almost like someone forcefully blotted out whatever was here," Kite said. "As if they just erased it."

"What do you mean, 'someone?' " I asked.

Kite looked at me. "Isn't it obvious?"

Only game administrators had that kind of power. It had to be someone at CC Corp.

But if they want something erased, they can erase it completely or use a protection to bar entry. So why hadn't they?

Whoever did this must have been in a panic and not done a thorough job. So what had been here that caused CC Corp. administrators to panic?

Then it hit me. *If they're the ones who make the game, why did they create whatever they tried to destroy here in the first place . . . ? Unless they didn't create it.* That's why they panicked. Someone else, someone outside of CC Corp., created whatever had been here.

I remembered Linda's words: *"The World isn't just some 'net game. There's something else with an agenda at work."*

"There's no point hanging around here. Let's go back to town," Kite said, sounding discouraged.

I understood his impatience. We'd run out of clues.

Everything Goes Wrong

I wanted to encourage him, but I knew how he felt all too well. There were times when you'd rather be left alone than listen to platitudes.

We returned to Mac•Anu in silence.

• ⬢ •

My exam scores were sporadic. *That's what I get for going to The World instead of studying.*

Now I had to figure out what to do with my test scores.

"Maybe I just won't tell my parents," I thought aloud.

No, that won't work. My dad's a teacher. Even though he worked at a different school, he knew I had exams. At least I hadn't flunked anything. So I went ahead and told them . . . and their reactions surprised me.

"We *have* been asking a lot of you these days," Mom said. "You've been looking after Kouta and helping us so much, it's understandable. Just keep trying your best." She put a light hand on my back.

"Too much tennis and not enough books," my dad said half-jokingly. "Well, I guess it's because you're so much like me. Don't worry—I'm sure you'll squeak by on your finals."

This didn't feel right. I almost wished they'd get mad at me. What he'd said to me before about him wanting to be stronger echoed in my head.

Don't blame yourself, Dad . . . this is just me reaping what I sowed.

When I entered Fumikazu's bedroom, Hana heard me and rushed over to her cage door, standing on her hind legs. I changed the straw for her bedding, gave her food, and refilled her drinking water. She looked thinner.

"You have to keep eating," I told her.

I often noticed her staring out the window at night, as if waiting for Fumikazu to come home.

My grunty in the game was just the opposite; it ate everything it could find.

Everything Goes Wrong

I first saw the thread labeled "MISSING" shortly before midterms. It was nothing more than messages exchanged between people searching for a player character named Alf.

Threads from people searching for absent companions weren't all that unusual; players sometimes just quit the game without telling their online friends. But something a friend of Alf wrote caught my eye and made me think that wasn't the case this time:

```
Alf wanted me to meet him there,
but when I tried to enter, it was
protected and I couldn't get in.
```

A place Alf used to visit was now protected, and he had disappeared. My mind raced. *What if Alf ran into a Data Bug and met with the same fate as Fumikazu?*

I sent an e-mail to Meg, who'd made the post.

```
I'd like to know more details about
your friend, if you're willing to tell
me.
```

Nearly a week passed before I had a reply, but Meg reluctantly consented to meet me. I promptly e-mailed Kite and we set out for the meeting place on Theta server at Great, Distant, Fertile Land.

Meg waited for us in the deepest part of the dungeon. We found her talking with a strange-looking character. His avatar resembled a typical merchant NPC that you'd find in a town, but there was never a character like that in a dungeon.

"Ah, there she is," Kite said. "But who's she with?"

"I don't know."

The second the merchant saw us, he warped out. *Could he have been a player?*

We approached Meg. I could see she was frightened.

"Who's that behind you?" she asked.

"He's a friend of mine. We're not here to try anything, so relax," I said, but she didn't. Something was out of place. "Meg? Where's the area Alf talked about?"

"Never mind," she said faintly, shaking her head.

"Never mind?"

She spoke quickly, panicked. "I shouldn't have posted on the BBS. I shouldn't have agreed to meet you."

She warped out.

When I checked the BBS later, her post had been deleted.

What happened to change her mind so quickly? Was it the merchant? Why was there an NPC in the dungeon? Could it have been a system administrator in disguise?

There were too many mysteries to unravel.

The sun shone brightly in the sky of Dun Loireag. My baby grunty continued demanding food for its bottomless stomach.

"Buheee!" it suddenly squealed and began to glow.

"What's wrong?!" I shouted.

"It's growing!" a voice said. I turned to see Chimney and Nova.

"See, look how big it's gotten." Chimney pointed toward my baby. My grunty now stood two sizes bigger than before.

I was stunned. "You see, grunties go through two growth phases before becoming adults," Nova explained.

"I'm surprised to see you raising one," Chimney said.

I explained how I'd accidentally bought it.

Chimney laughed. "You're pretty spacy, BlackRose."

"Never mind that. How come you're here?"

"We were walking by when Chimney noticed you standing around," Nova said.

"I shouted, but you didn't notice," said Chimney.

I scrolled back through the log. He *had* called out. "Sorry."

Chimney moved closer. "A lot's been happening in this game lately."

"You said it. Do you read the BBS, BlackRose?" asked Nova.

"I skim it," I answered.

"I don't read it at all," said Chimney indifferently. "I just ask Nova about it."

It was funny to see how different these two were.

"I was just reading about how Orca of the Azure Sea hasn't logged on lately," Nova said. "That's big news, since he's usually here every day."

I couldn't tell them Orca *couldn't* log in because he was in a coma from playing the game. No one else knew that.

"Orca of the Azure Sea?" said Chimney. "Isn't he one of the Descendants of Fianna?"

"Right," Nova continued. "He's famous for clearing the The One Sin event with Balmung."

Finally, I remembered where I'd heard of them before. *Fumikazu mentioned them right before he went into a coma.*

I wished I could talk to Fumikazu, even if just to tell him I was trying my best. Although I was up against a foe so formidable that it beat one of the two greatest heroes the game had ever produced, I would still *try* to fight it.

I decided to see if I could influence my new friends. "Oh yeah, I heard a lot of people are leaving the game lately," I said casually.

"Is that true?" Chimney asked.

"Is it because of the kid who fell into a coma?" Nova replied.

My heart jumped. *Are they talking about my brother?* "What kid?" I asked.

"Some high school senior. I heard about it in the news."

They were talking about someone else. *How many people have been affected so far?!*

"So what? You're not scared, are you?" Chimney taunted.

I looked up the article on a different screen while we talked. The senior's name was Tomonari Kasumi; he was from Kanazawa. The article said he collapsed in a gaming club office with a friend, who also fainted but quickly recovered.

What if the two of them had been playing The World? But why did one fall into a coma, while the other recovered? What made their fates different? As long as I knew there was a chance for recovery, I had to keep moving forward.

"That coma thing kind of reminds me of something I read on the BBS about The Fragment," Chimney said.

"The Fragment?" I asked. "What's that?"

"It's the original version of The World," Nova explained. "There was a rumor on the message boards that one of the original thousand players of The Fragment committed suicide just before the game ended."

"Oh my goodness!" I cried.

"Yeah, pretty tragic. I'm sure it didn't have anything to do with the game. His life must have been crud before that," Chimney added.

"Wait, how do you know that isn't just a rumor someone started?" I said. "You know, like getting an A on all your college exams if your roommate dies."

Nova shrugged. "Well, that's what the BBS threads were saying, at least . . . except now that I think about it, maybe it was a programmer." He cocked his head to the side.

"One of the programmers committed suicide?"

"Actually, I think he just disappeared. I don't remember. I read it so long ago," Nova said. "But I don't think they ever found him, so everyone assumed he died."

"But really, he's just missing?"

"Yeah, I guess."

I would have to investigate further. *If The Fragment is the previous version of The World, is the same programmer responsible for the current problems?*

"You don't happen to know his name, do you?" I pressed.

"Why are you so interested?" asked Chimney.

"I'm just concerned. I didn't think a game could have such deadly consequences," I *tried* to say matter-of-factly.

"They're just rumors. And rumors are best when they end quickly," Chimney announced pointedly.

"True. We can't have fun playing if we believe all the rumors," added Nova.

I wished they were only rumors, but I knew better. At least now, I had a new lead to investigate.

"Oh, look! Isn't that the cat character everyone's talking about?"

I followed Chimney's gaze to a suspension bridge. For the first time, I witnessed the strange feline. *Is this the character Kite talked about meeting?*

She had indigo fur, and long ears that were actually more rabbit-like than feline. She appeared to be a Blademaster, although I didn't know if she could be counted as that class anymore.

"She can't be a player," Nova commented. "She must be an NPC, because players can't create avatars that look like animals."

I couldn't take my eyes off her. *What's her name again? Mia?* "Maybe she's an administrator?"

"She's coming this way," Nova pointed out.

Mia steadily approached us. A sinking feeling formed in my gut. There were no other characters in sight, and I doubted she was heading to the grunty ranch.

I knew she couldn't be an NPC. She had been in a party with Elk. I didn't think she was an administrator either. An administrator wasn't likely to tell Kite about gate-hacking.

She looked directly at me. "I wonder if we could speak alone," she said. Her words were so unexpected, I didn't react.

"Do you know her?" Nova asked.

"N-no," I stammered.

"You can decline if you want," Nova said, stepping forward to shield me.

Mia just continued to gaze at me with her big eyes, as if Nova and Chimney weren't there. "Come along. I'll show you something you'll want to see." Without waiting for an answer, she walked toward the Chaos Gate.

"Sorry. I need to go," I told my friends.

"What?! Don't go with her!" Chimney protested.

"Do you want us to go with you?" Nova asked.

I did, but I couldn't involve them. "I'll be all right! Leave it to me! Don't worry."

I quickly ran after Mia. When I caught up with her, she suddenly turned and said, "You smell like the bracelet. Do you know the bracelet's owner?"

"Huh?"

"I can smell it on you."

What is she talking about? How can she smell anything in a game?

"Want to know where we're going?" she asked, her eyes blazing. "You'll go, won't you?"

I nodded as if hypnotized. Of course I would go. It was the only way to find out why Fumikazu collapsed and how he might recover.

I passed my member address to her and we formed a party.

We transferred to the Delta server and went to Bursting, Passed Over, Aqua Field. It was a newbie area with an estimated level of 1.

Why are we here?

Suddenly, everything rumbled so loudly that I wanted to cover my ears. The display flashed blindingly white.

"What's going on?!" I yelled.

When I opened my eyes, Mia had disappeared. A wilderness stretched before me. Pieces of ruins and rocky crags floated in the dark green sky. A pale mist hung over the ground.

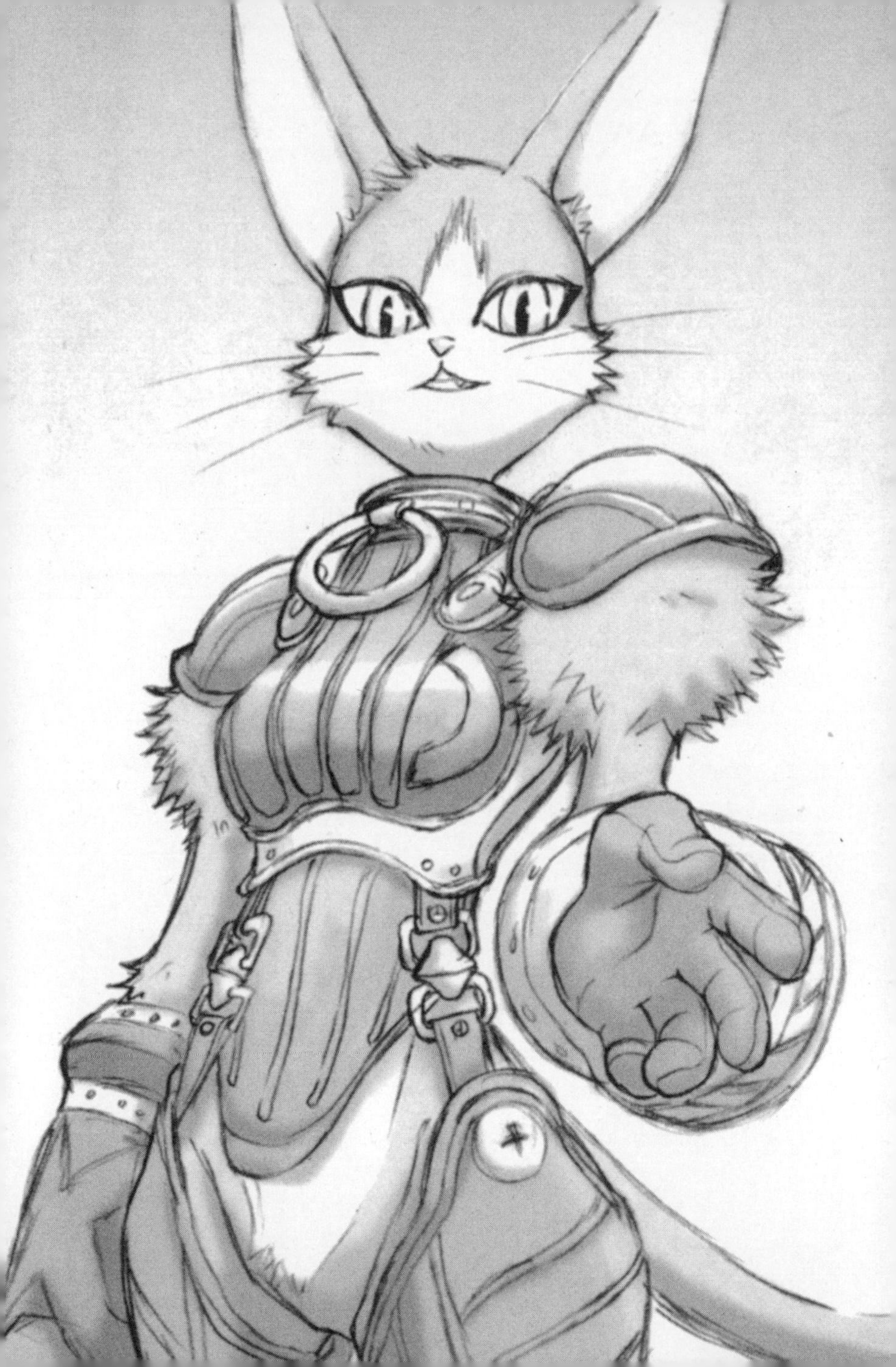

I could see a magic portal faintly drawn at my feet; the color matched the tear in the graphics.

I tried to swallow, but my mouth was too dry.

I heard an eerie noise behind me. Quickly, I turned. The graphics inverted, rippling and warping into a circular shape.

A red cross emerged from the sunken center of the disc. It was different from a typical cross, in that the intersection held a circle. I knew I'd seen it somewhere before, but I wasn't sure what kind of cross it was.

"Stay away!" I shouted.

I felt goose bumps run up and down my arms.

From inside the warped space, the thing holding the red cross slowly appeared. It was humanoid, with skin the texture of rock, and it emanated a black, ominous aura.

It looked like Death.

Suddenly I *knew* that this was the thing that put Fumikazu into a coma.

It was coming straight at me. *But without Kite, how can I defeat it?*

Crush

"Come on and fight!"

I was actually impressed with my bravado. Unfortunately, the creature continued to approach, brandishing the cross before my eyes.

I wanted to run, but there was nowhere to go. Even though defeating it was impossible, I readied my sword.

The creature floated in the air, raising its red cross. I suddenly felt like I had a gun aimed at my head.

This is supposed to be only a game, I told myself.

Slowly, it raised its other arm. Light focused sharply as it concentrated its ghastly power.

This thing is going to get me! I've got to move! I've got to do something right now!

The more I panicked, the less I knew what to do. I was paralyzed by fear.

I'm going to end up like Fumikazu, I thought.

Fumikazu. As the image of his sleeping face crystallized, something deep inside me began to boil.

I won't lie down and die without a fight!

"Give me back Fumikazu!" I shouted.

I jumped in the air and slashed at it. I might only have one chance, so I aimed at the shoulder and swung using all my might.

The sword passed right through the creature as if it were made of air. I went right through it as well, and then landed somewhere behind it.

I sensed another presence behind me. *What now?!*

I spun around to face a character I'd never seen before. He was ginormous, with blue-painted skin and hair that partially concealed his face. Crucified on the cross that Death had been holding, he slowly rose into the air.

Then another form appeared. I couldn't believe my eyes. It was Kite!

I tried to meet him halfway, but my body wouldn't move; my legs were stuck to the ground.

Then I realized that none of this was real. That's why I couldn't interfere. *It's an illusion.* I was watching the past replay before my eyes.

Suddenly, it all made sense. The victim on the cross must have been Kite's friend, Orca. All I could do was watch as the scene unfolded.

Everything moved in slow motion. A dazzling arrow of light flew from Death's arm toward Orca on the cross. He was being Data Drained.

I stiffened.

The light zapped Orca and he fell with a thud. He didn't move. I could hear Orca groaning as Kite tried to run toward him.

"It wasn't supposed to be this way. I'm sorry. Get out of here!" Orca gasped.

Orca's body rose into the air, and suddenly his image dispersed. All the data that formed him disassembled. *Data Drain!* This was the moment a player lost consciousness!

Before I could get everything straight in my head, the image disappeared, swallowed in a sea of noise and light.

There was a thick, dull sound, and then everything went black.

"SYSTEM ERROR" flashed on the screen. I'd been kicked out of The World.

I flung the goggles from my head; my body was soaked in sweat. I closed my eyes and breathed deeply.

I heard an ambulance siren rushing somewhere down the street. It sent a shiver through me.

I looked down and noticed an orange light spilling from the goggles. I timidly peeked inside and saw The World desktop.

Even the system error had been an illusion.

I noticed the e-mail icon flashing on and off. I had a message from Mia.

You just witnessed the instant your friend received the bracelet. The human who was Data Drained is in a coma. You wanted to see that, didn't you? Let's keep this a secret between us. Of course, I don't think anyone else would believe you if you told them.

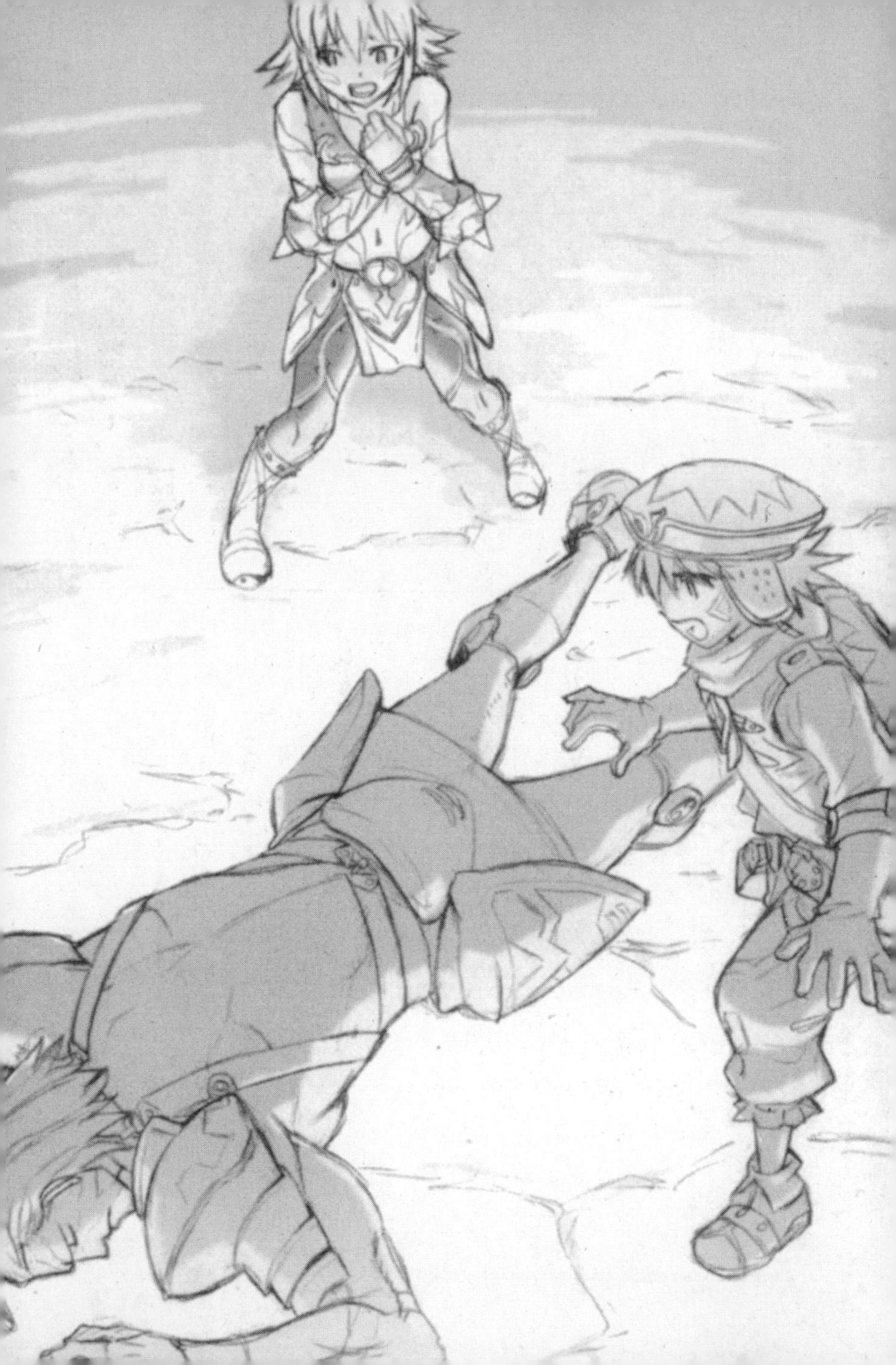

I reread the e-mail again and again.

Should I tell Kite? He's the only one who would believe me. But I was sure Kite didn't want to relive the bitter memory, so I decided not to tell him.

But why did Mia show me what happened? And how was she able to show it to me?

More important, who is Mia?

I tried to write a reply to Mia's message, but no matter how many times I sent it, it bounced back.

• ⬢ •

Even though it was fall, the air remained thick with summer heat. Everyone seemed calm, but I couldn't stop my heart from pounding and my legs from shaking. This would be my first tournament.

I trudged along, the last in line, as I headed toward the courts. I saw Risa with the upperclassmen. They looked in my direction. I tried to meet her eyes, but she quickly looked away.

I wanted her to help me, but I knew that if she was seen talking to me, she'd be bullied too.

Crush

I couldn't think about it. I had to concentrate on the match. Bullying was outside the court, and I couldn't let it interfere with my game.

But I knew it would only get worse if I lost. They would say that I couldn't handle it, that I shouldn't have been given a position on the team. I had to do well in today's match to prove myself.

I stood alone on the courts. No one wanted to do warm-up stretches with me. Koura and Asaoka were busy setting up, so I stretched alone.

At times, I felt Risa looking at me, but I didn't acknowledge her.

"Hayami?" Captain Koura called. I rushed over.

"It's mostly team games today, so don't worry too much. I know it's your first match, so just do your best." She gave me a friendly smile.

"I will!"

The tournament would last two days. Today we would do doubles, singles, then doubles again. A match would end once someone won two sets. Tomorrow would be all individual matches.

"Let's head on over to the court," urged Koura.

My right hand shook. I told myself it would be all right, that I'd trained hard for this.

The court felt bigger now that it was surrounded by a sea of eager faces. Staring out at the spectators, I had a sudden sensation of vertigo.

"Hayami?" Asaoka called.

"Yes?" I answered, my throat dry.

"Are you ready for your first formal match?"

"Hayami can handle it, right?" Koura patted me on the back.

I nodded. The coach grinned as he sat on the bench.

"I'm sure you'll do fine," he said reassuringly.

Yeah, I can do this.

I sat through the first few matches, my mind completely blank, until Asaoka snapped me out of it.

"You should go warm up," she urged.

I looked around the crowd. My dad had said he would come. I hoped that he'd stayed home, but I knew he wouldn't. He was probably out there somewhere, waiting to cheer me on. I only hoped I wouldn't disappoint him.

The whistle signaled the end of the first doubles match, and my body lurched.

Crush

Koura and Amemiya worked in perfect unison and nearly shut out the opposing team.

"Hayami, your shoes are untied," Asaoka called out as I headed toward the court.

I bent down to tie them. My hands started shaking as I remembered how the laces had gotten cut the day the bullying began.

Calm down, I told myself. *Stay focused. Nothing matters but the game.*

"Hayami!" the coach shouted before I reached the court.

"Yes, sir?"

"Relax."

"Yes, sir!" I answered.

I felt dazed. I couldn't even hear the cheers from the crowd. I had to win this match.

I faced my opponent, who was serving first. Asaoka had told me she was a junior who'd won second place at last year's spring tournament. Her specialty was using her long reach in volleys.

Our eyes met for an instant. Cold sweat dripped down my back.

Stay focused!

I tightened my grip on my racket and took a deep breath. *I can do this.* The referee blew the whistle; my opponent's first serve blistered down the middle. I returned badly, and she scored the point. *She's a good player. That's okay. I don't have to break her serve right away—just focus on not letting her break mine.*

She won the first game, but I managed to calm down enough to hold serve on the second. It was an adequate start—I just had to get into a good rhythm and hope that an opportunity would come up later in the set.

Back and forth it went until we'd each won four. But just as she went up to serve the ninth game, I saw my dad waving from outside the fence.

In that instant, my opponent's smash blew right by me. An ace.

"Fifteen–love."

Why did he have to show up?

Suddenly it was as if nothing I did was right. My dad's presence there rattled me. *C'mon—you're first string! First stringers shouldn't let simple stuff like that bug them!* But no, the fact that it had affected me rattled me even more, and I lost the next point as well. Then when I managed to get the next point on a lucky shot, I couldn't help thinking that first-stringers shouldn't have to rely on luck!

I knew it didn't make any sense, but I started to feel like all the people watching me knew what those bullies on the team had been saying behind my back—that I, a freshman, didn't deserve to be playing that game. And when the next three points blew by me, it only reinforced my feelings of unworthiness.

Losing that game should have been nothing big, but just thinking about it completely ruined my rhythm, and I only managed one point in the next game. My serve was broken, and with that, the first set belonged to my opponent.

Almost drowned by the cheers of the students and parents from the other school came the sound of Koura's voice. He said that the match was only just beginning, but his words didn't really reach my heart. All I could think about was how if I lost the next set, it'd be over. I'd fail my school, and there would be no end to those whispers behind my back. I clenched my teeth.

Then I heard someone shout my name. It was Miho! Shouko stood next to her, waving. Somehow seeing their familiar faces and school uniforms helped me collect my scattered wits and calm my nerves. I realized it didn't really make any sense that this should calm me, when seeing my dad had rattled me, but somehow it was enough to allow me to go out there and serve a good first game of the second set. It was on the next game that my opportunity came.

My opponent served—too soft. Her mistake. I rushed the net and smashed it back.

Love–15. I still had a chance.

I had strength and endurance. My technique and strategy weren't so hot, but if I could rally until my opponent ran out of stamina, I could still win. Whatever she hit at me, I would wear her down physically. It was the only weapon I had.

Love–30 . . . Love–40 . . . Maybe it wasn't the most impressive display of tennis skills to watch, but I got the job done. Her serve was broken, and I was up two games to none.

My serve. I was fine. Now the only cheers I let get through to me were from my supporters—my friends, and my dad. Three games to zero. After that, I just focused again on holding serve. Second set, victory.

"Yes!" I finally allowed myself to show some emotion.

"That's good, Hayami. Put all your energy into it." My coach sounded confident, but I knew I had gotten there more out of sheer doggedness than actual skill. Still, I grinned almost savagely and took a swig of my sports drink before settling in for the next set.

So what if it's not pretty? I'll just keep wearing her down, and we'll see who comes out on top.

She started the third set, and we again traded off holding serve. In my fourth service game, she managed to get ahead on the first point with her trademark smash return, but it had lost its edge. Before my next serve, I stared across the net at my opponent's face. She was breathing heavily—the long match had obviously taken a toll on her.

She did manage to return my next serve, but it came back as a dull lob. I smashed it back, managing a bit of a spin on the ball, and she couldn't get to it in time. It was 15–15 . . .

So what if she'd gotten the first point? She had definitely run out of energy—but I still had a lot of game left!

If she scores, I'll just score back, and then after winning this game, I'll take advantage of her fatigue and break her next serve.

My next serve was a winner, but then the next volley was intense. I fired off powerful shots, shots that were hard to hit, but she managed to keep returning them.

"Hayami, keep going!"

Wait. Was that voice . . . Risa's?

Our eyes met briefly through the fence. The upperclassmen around her whispered to her, but she ignored them. Perhaps my other friends' cheers for me had given her courage. The sound of her voice spread warmth to my chest, and I nodded to her. The intense game occupied all my attention, but right then I must have been smiling.

I'm fine now. Everything's going to be okay.

But then I overreached; my return went a bit long, and my opponent had tied the game. On her next return it looked like she was drawing on her very last reserves, and I had to hit back frantically to keep from being left behind. But this had to be her final effort. *I'm definitely going to be able to win this!*

But the instant I thought that, she swung left and I ran to cover—but the ball came right. It was a feint! She was up, and she feinted on her next return also, breaking my serve. She *was* more fatigued than me, and it

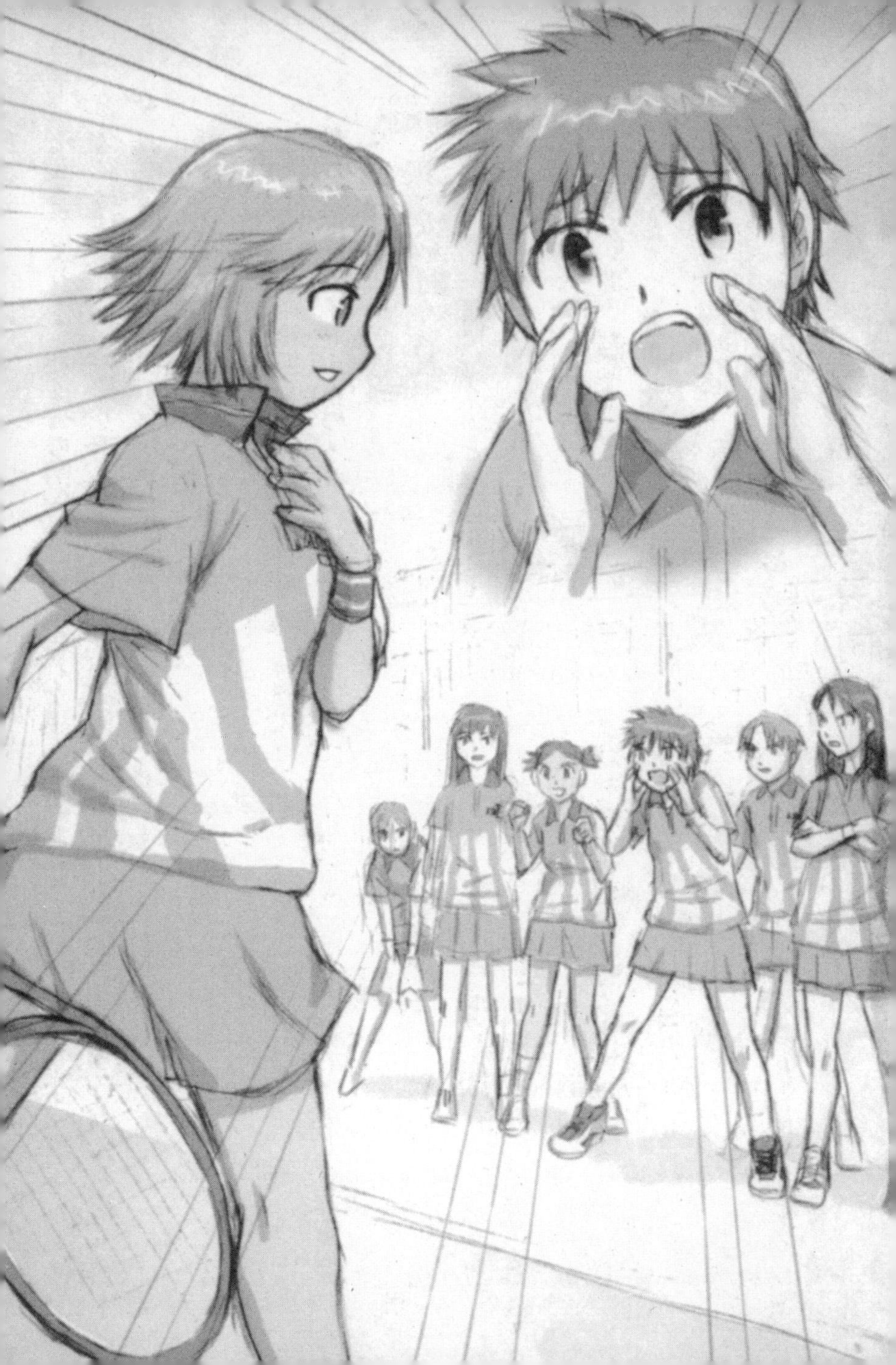

must have been obvious to everyone watching—but so was our difference in skill level. She'd finally found my Achilles' heel, and she took advantage of it on feint after feint. I just kept falling for it, until on match point I broke the other way expecting a feint—and it ended up a straight shot that rushed behind me.

I had lost. A tear of frustration rolled down my cheek. *I tried so hard and still lost!*

We traded respectful bows across the net, and she smiled at me. "You just about had me," she let out, obviously drained. "Your stamina is amazing. But it takes experience to recognize feints—I'm sure you'll get there before long. That was a good match."

I nodded. It still hurt, but she was right. At least now I knew my weakness. I could improve. I *would* improve.

After my match, our second doubles team unexpectedly lost as well, handing our high school a first-round loss and early exit from the tournament. And then in my double-elimination individual tournament matches the next day, both of my opponents exploited my now widely known weakness against feints and took me down in rather short order, leaving me with a very bitter taste in my mouth. But

I did start to see the feints a bit better by the end of the second game, though still not nearly well enough to pull out a victory.

My experience in the tournament gave me a burning desire to get better. I now knew the exact skills that I lacked.

And I did take one thing away from the tournament that made me more than happy enough to overcome the disappointment. Risa had called out to me. She was still my friend. And now our relationship was back to normal. It had been so long since she and I had made our trip home side by side, but now we talked about places we wanted to go, things we wanted to shop for . . . meaningless little things that meant everything in the world to me.

●◆●

I had an e-mail from Kite.

    I know where it is. I've finally found it!

He didn't say anything else. Was the "it" he referred to the Death-thing I'd witnessed? He didn't say what he was going to do now that he'd found it, but he clearly didn't invite me along. It was obvious that he wanted to do this alone.

I logged on to look for him. Since he wasn't there yet, I lingered near the Theta server Chaos Gate, unable to get Orca's words out of my head: *"It wasn't supposed to be this way. I'm sorry. Get out of here!"*

I think Orca must have been teaching Kite about the game, just as Nova and Chimney had showed me. Once they'd encountered the irregular creature, Orca had tried to protect Kite, and in the end had been forced to use himself as a shield so Kite could escape.

Kite appeared from the Chaos Gate and froze. "Oh, hey."

"Were you going to go without me?" I asked angrily.

"It might be there," he said hoarsely. "The thing that hurt Orca. I didn't want to put you at risk, too."

I wasn't going to ask where he'd learned his information. It didn't bother me if he investigated when I wasn't around, but when it came to confronting the creature that had brought us together, we were in this to the end. "Are you going to try and defeat it?"

"I don't know if I can," he said glumly.

"I'm going with you." *I might not be much use in the fight, but I can't let him go alone.*

Kite remained quiet.

"What's wrong?" I asked.

He hesitated. "It's dangerous."

"So what?" I replied. "Hasn't that been the case the whole time? I won't let you leave me here after we've come this far."

Kite remained silent before he finally replied, "If you're that determined—"

"Then let's get going," I finished his sentence.

We formed a party.

"So where's the enemy?"

"At Chosen—"

He was about to tell me when I heard a familiar voice.

"Heeeeey! Where are you two going?"

Kite and I turned around.

"Mistral!"

"Smells to me like something's up. Take me with you!"

I didn't like the idea of bringing her along. She didn't know the risks like I did.

"Not today, Mistral," Kite replied.

I'm glad for once we're on the same page.

"Anywhere you go, you'll need a Wavemaster, you know," Mistral insisted. "C'mon, hurry and invite me."

Kite and I switched to party chat so we could talk privately.

"What do we do?" I asked.

"We could use a Wavemaster, but it's too dangerous."

"You said it."

Kite switched back and told Mistral, "I'm sorry, Mistral, this is a game, but we're going someplace really dangerous."

"Dangerous? Am I too low-level for you?"

"It's not that."

Mistral's voice suddenly sounded gleeful. "If it has something to do with that room we visited, then I think I have a right to go, too."

Kite and I looked at each other.

"You sure you want to go?" Kite asked.

"Of course," she replied.

I sighed. "I guess we don't want word of this spreading," I told Kite privately.

"All right," said Kite. "You're in, on one condition. If it gets too dangerous, you have to drop out of the party and run."

"Ho ho! This sounds juicy." Mistral grinned.

"I'm not kidding. Agreed?" he pressed.

"Okay, okay!"

Kite invited Mistral into the party.

"So, let's gooo!"

Kite looked in my direction and nodded. "The place we're going to is called Chosen, Hopeless, Nothingness."

"Sounds lovely," I commented.

The transfer screen changed to a gate-hacking screen. I wondered if we'd make it back unharmed.

"What is this place?" asked Mistral.

A howling wind pierced my ears. As I looked around, I could see a bunch of short barren trees lit against the twilight sky. Bleached bones sat in piles beneath their trunks. A deep, swirling black fog covered the ground, though small fissures opened up to reveal dark red magma. Whenever the light from the magma faded, computer code crackled up.

This was a bad place.

There were many rifts in the scenery, far more than any other place I had visited, with the exception of the scene Mia had shown me.

"The bracelet," muttered Kite.

"Does it hurt?" I asked.

"No. It's shining."

Kite's bracelet pulsed with energy. "This is the first time it's done that," he added.

"Hey, hey, there's a dungeon over there." Mistral came running up. I hadn't even noticed she'd left.

"Were you walking around?" Kite asked.

"Yup. I had to check it out. I mean, this is one unusual area, right?"

"Try and stay close from now on," Kite warned.

"Fine, but can we hit the dungeon already?" Mistral pleaded.

"Yeah, let's go!"

We ran into several magic portals, all of them filled with powerful enemies. We tried to keep our contact to a minimum so we'd be fresh for whatever we faced underground.

Crush

The dungeon walls, floor, and ceiling contained the same fissures and tears in the fabric of the game as everywhere else. I renewed my grip on the controller. We couldn't go back now.

We saw the familiar purple mist just outside the final room. Mistral cast boosting magic on us before we entered. This way we were stronger, tougher, and faster than ever.

"It's a boss or something, right? With this magic boost, we should kick ass," Mistral said with a grin.

But I knew boosting magic wouldn't protect us from a Data Drain.

I wiped the sweat from my hands onto my shirt. "Let's go."

Kite took the lead and advanced slowly into the room. Mistral and I followed behind.

"What the heck *is* this place?!" Mistral shouted.

It no longer looked like a room, but more like an entirely new location. I recognized it as the place where Orca had fallen. When we walked through the door, we must have warped from the dungeon to this location.

A pretty young girl in a white dress floated in the air. She looked familiar as well.

"Aura?!" Kite cried.

She's the one who gave Kite his bracelet, I thought. Then I realized where I had seen her—it was her statue bound at the altar in Hidden, Forbidden, Holy Ground. That's why Kite had examined the statue so closely—he'd recognized her.

"I see you received my message." Aura's voice was quiet, as if coming from far away. "Unfortunately, it's too late."

Did Aura tell Kite where to find the Death-thing?

"Wait! There's something I have to ask you!" As Kite spoke, Aura started fading, becoming almost transparent— and then a red cross suddenly appeared behind her.

"Whazzat?" cried Mistral.

The scenery inverted and the piercing howl returned.

Death!

I wanted to run, but I stood my ground.

It raised its hands over its head, pointing at Aura.

"Nooooo!" Kite cried.

Before we could do anything, it fired a Data Drain at her. Her body scattered and disappeared; only a crimson sphere remained, hanging in the air like a red balloon.

Aura's spirit?

Death's body contracted as it amassed power. Flickering lightning shot from its hands. Then it surged its power at the red ball of light. We heard Aura's terrified scream as her core split into three pieces and then disappeared into the sky.

Aura was gone, and so was any clue that she might have given us.

I gazed at Death. Its ominous red cross shined in my eyes.

"Here it comes!"

We readied our weapons. Behind us, Mistral backed away.

"A boss like this might use long-range attacks after all," she explained shakily.

It seemed even more overwhelming than when I saw it the other day. Somehow I suddenly knew its name was Skeith.

Huh? How do I know that? Then I remembered the names written on the pedestal of the girl's statue: Skeith . . . Innis . . . Magus . . .

"BlackRose!" Kite shouted.

Skeith charged directly at me.

It moved with such speed, I couldn't avoid it. It struck me with so much force that a shudder wracked my body and made me jerk in my computer chair.

My avatar's hit points dropped to nearly zero in an instant. But then I heard Mistral chant an Ol Repth recovery spell behind me, and my health meter returned to normal.

Doing a somersault to gather force, I swung my Heavy Blade down as hard as I could.

"Death bringer!" I shouted.

Skeith's health meter barely dropped.

Whatever this thing was, it was tough!

Without pausing, Kite and I launched another assault.

Skeith's red cross moved behind me. It rose into the air to crucify me as it had Orca.

"No!" Kite slashed, but it didn't even twitch.

It happened in an instant. Light shot from Skeith's hand. My avatar fell to the ground with a thud.

Again, my health verged on death. Everything flickered, indicating that I had been afflicted with virtually every game malady: paralysis, poison, slow, and sleep. Yet somehow I could still move. *Is this the grace of the bracelet that Mia talked about?* At any rate, I was saved; the Data Drain was ineffective!

Kite rushed over and used an item on me. First one, then all of the afflictions vanished.

"You okay?"

"I'm fine," I murmured, readying my Heavy Blade.

Mistral cast Vak Kruz, and a ring of light green fireballs converged on Skeith.

"Hey, what's that?" I asked, pointing.

An icon reading "Protect Break OK" appeared next to Skeith's figure after Mistral's attack hit.

Kite clutched the bracelet. "Now it's my turn." I guessed that meant the Data Drain would only work on an opponent after the "Protect Break OK" status appeared.

Now it was up to Kite. If his Data Drain didn't work or he missed, the three of us would end up like Fumikazu and Orca.

"You ready?" I asked Kite.

"Ready!" He got into position.

Skeith noticed Kite's movements, but I blocked Skeith's path as it moved toward Kite.

I couldn't let it interfere. "*I'm* the one you're fighting!"

Mistral cast a barrage of recovery magic on me to keep me alive.

I threw my few remaining skill points into one all-or-nothing attack.

Then, from over my shoulder, a ray of light shot out—Kite's Data Drain. It pierced straight through Skeith.

A thunderous sound roared—as if the very earth were rumbling. Skeith suddenly changed form. Its body transformed into solid stone. It became a rock!

But it was no ordinary rock. Creepy characters bubbled up from its stony surface.

"Is *this* Skeith's true form?" I asked.

It was easier to attack now, so we slowly whittled away Skeith's hit points. Because Mistral didn't need to constantly cast recovery spells, she was able to get in on the action, throwing offensive magic at the creature. Spells I'd never seen before flew past me.

"We can do it!" Kite screamed.

"Calamity!" I shouted, launching an attack skill. I slashed the stone from top to bottom with my Heavy Blade. It looked like one more strike would kill it.

"Gale of Swords!" Kite yelled as he unleashed a number of slashes at a dizzying speed.

Skeith fell.

"We did it," I cried.

"Yeah."

Mistral ran up and joined us. "We got him!"

All monsters, once they were defeated, were supposed to disappear, but Skeith's body started dissolving into slime.

"That's weird," I said.

"What's wrong?" asked Mistral.

I pointed to the slime. Suddenly, the screen went dark. Everything started rumbling. An erratic *zzzzt* came from everywhere, like something short-circuiting.

Skeith's corpse finished dissolving and turned into a black shadow; it bubbled like it was boiling. Giant, pointed tree-shapes poked through the blackened ground and towered up from every direction. We were surrounded!

I dropped the controller and grabbed the goggles with both hands. Scared, I closed my eyes.

All sound suddenly ceased. I slowly opened my eyes.

The boiling black shadow and the trees that had grown from it were gone.

Kite surveyed our surroundings while Mistral stood frozen to the spot—for once, speechless.

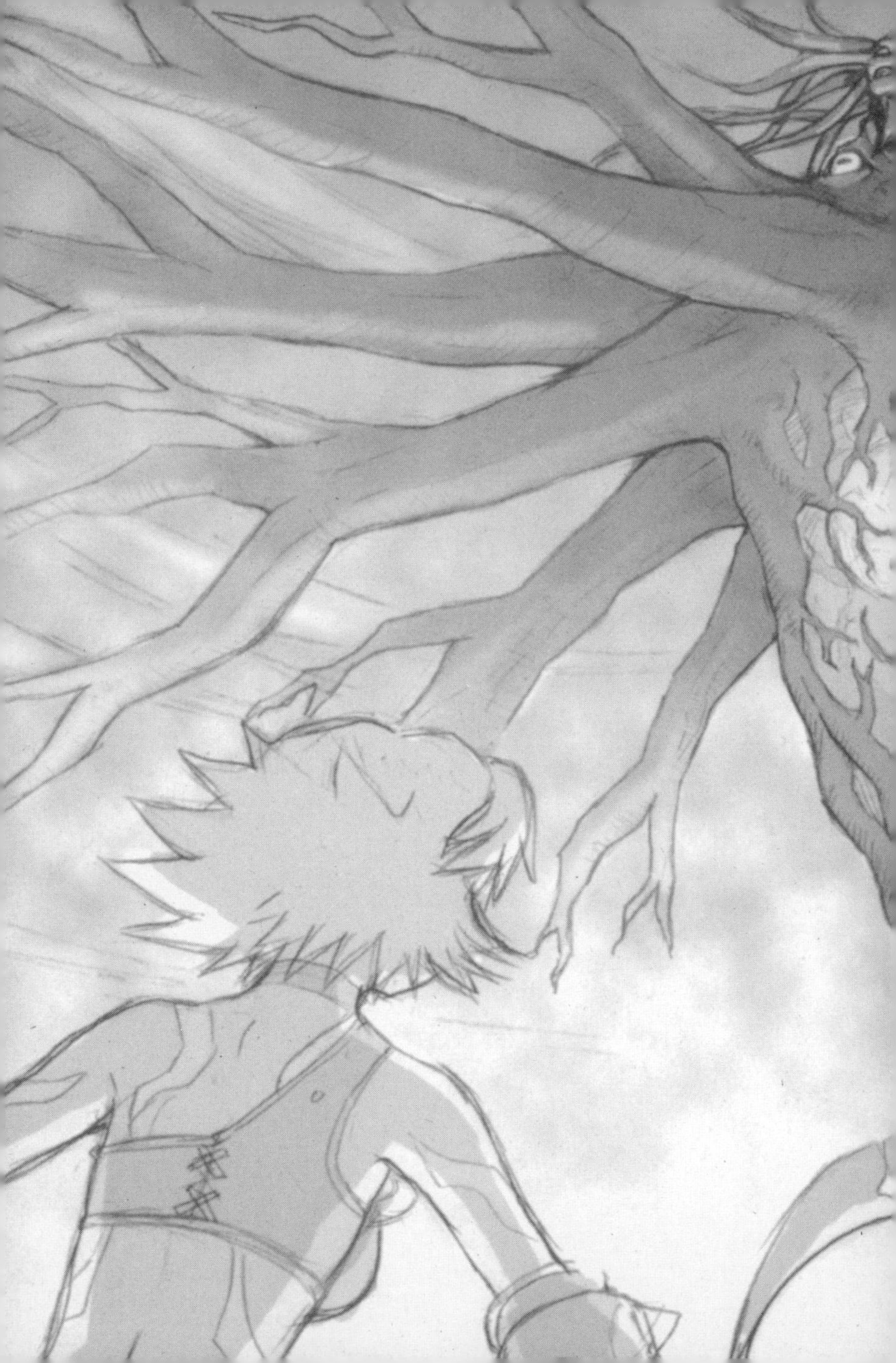

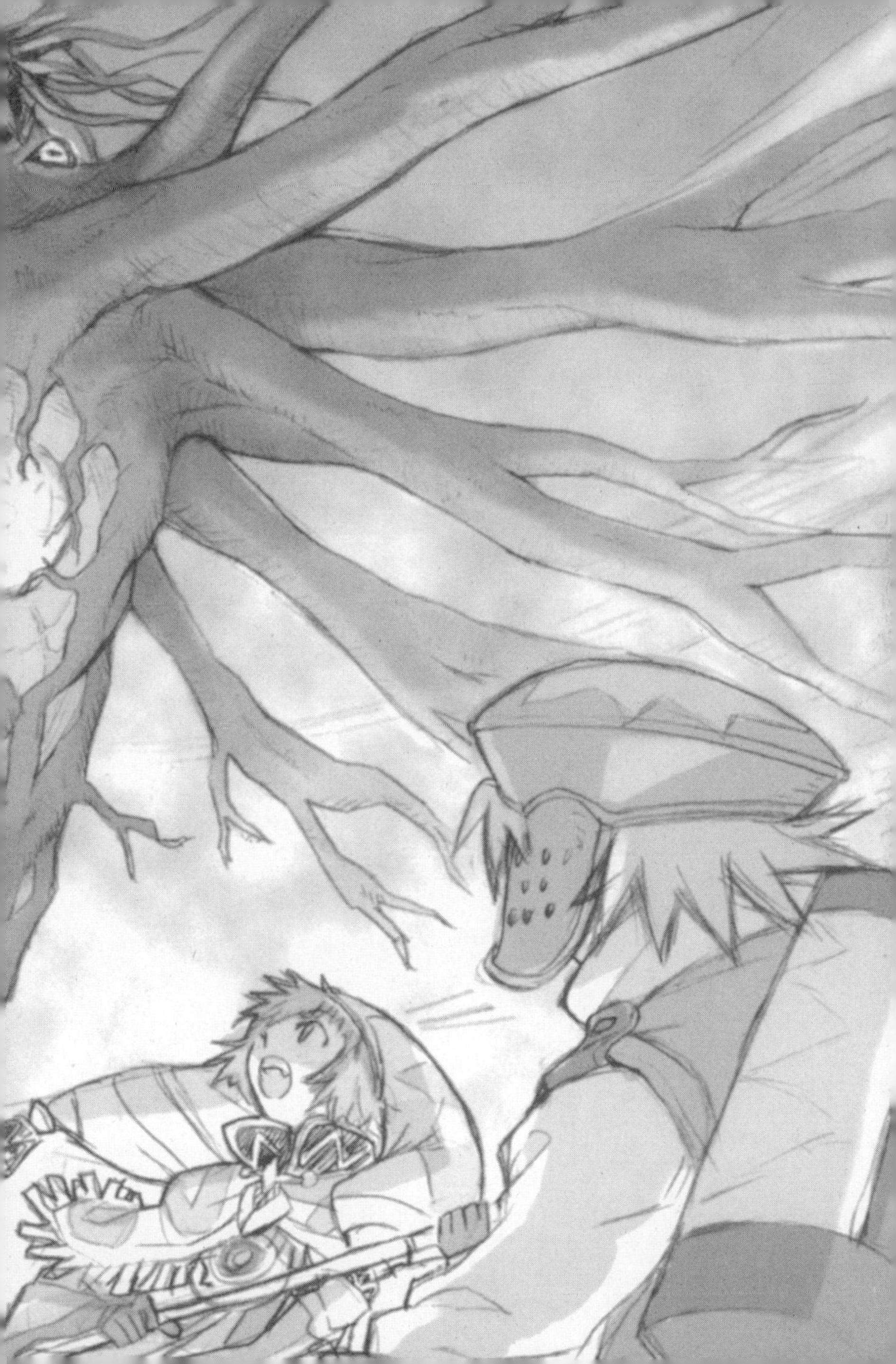

I tried to move, then remembered I'd dropped the controller. Reaching for it, I noticed Kite's dumbfounded gaze.

I recovered the controller and looked up.

High above us was a giant monstrous creature, its entire body comprised of what looked like twisty pale-blue tree roots. Surrounded by the erratic pattern of roots was a red solid core pulsating like a heartbeat.

The next instant, the air rippled and shook with tremendous force. We were thrown to the ground, helpless against its attack. All it did was speak. The incredible force that hit us was nothing *more* than its voice.

I fell unconscious.

The Next Stage

SYSTEM ERROR!
SYSTEM ERROR!
SYSTEM ERROR!

The two words flashed repeatedly on my display. I rubbed my head. It felt like I'd been out for days, but when I checked the clock, it had only been five minutes.

I had no idea what happened. *Are Kite and Mistral okay?* I wanted to know, but I was afraid to return to find out. Nevertheless, I had to. But when I tried to reenter The World, I couldn't get in. Server trouble.

Instead of sleeping, I waited for the server to come back up. It was almost dawn by the time the problem was fixed and I could finally log back on.

I found an unusually high number of posts on the BBS. I read as many as I could.

Many of the posts described a terrible noise, followed by the connection dropping. Panic spread as rumors of a deadly virus infiltrating the server were posted everywhere.

We'd defeated Skeith, but I wondered if doing so hadn't just created a bigger mess.

While reading the BBS, I received an e-mail from Mistral. She was okay. I drew a long sigh of relief and opened the message.

```
Who knew there were monsters like
that? Let's play again sometime!
(*^_^*)
```

Ugh. Figures. She was clueless. Despite everything that had happened, she thought it was all part of the game.

That left Kite. If Mistral and I were okay, I'm sure he was too. The only one who had been hurt was Aura.

Skeith . . . Innis . . . Magus . . .

Now that Skeith was defeated, could the creepy tree thing that had bubbled out of Skeith's shadow and risen monstrously to the sky have been Innis? In either case, it wasn't over yet. Both Innis and Magus had to be dealt with, not to mention the other monsters whose names had been scraped off the pedestal.

I knew the server crash had to be related to Skeith's defeat as well, but I didn't know how. I e-mailed Kite:

I can't help but worry—are you okay?

Did we cause the server to crash? I hope everything returns to normal soon. What we did was a good thing, wasn't it?

—BlackRose

● ◆ ●

"Miho and I were online when we thought we heard a weird voice, and then the connection dropped," Shouko said excitedly. "What do you think it was?"

"I just hope it wasn't the virus everyone's talking about," said Miho.

I felt guilty knowing they were both playing the game at the moment of Skeith's defeat.

"If it's a virus, isn't that a good reason to quit playing?" I asked.

"But it's just a game," said Miho indifferently.

I used to think that, too, but now I know better. It's not only real, it's deadly. Just ask my brother.

I wanted to tell them about everything that had happened, but I couldn't. Even if I did, they wouldn't believe me. They didn't even think I played online games.

Shouko changed the subject. "Enough about the game. Tell us about your match, Akira!"

"Yeah, I didn't know you were so good!" Miho smiled.

"What do you mean? I lost," I replied.

"Yeah, but you kicked ass in that second set. And all your matches were close. I think you were just nervous."

"That's right. Akira's our ace in the hole."

I turned to see who had spoken, and there was Risa standing behind us, smiling.

I grinned. Those upperclassmen were still probably grumbling about me from the shadows, but it no longer bothered me.

Shouko noticed the look that passed between us and gave a smile of her own.

• ⬡ •

I gazed at the Chaos Gate. I wanted to see what had happened afterward, but I couldn't do it alone.

I shifted the goggles so I could see the clock in my room. Kite usually showed up on time, but I was always early. I wondered what Kite was doing right now in real life. *Does he have a job? Does he go to school?*

"Found ya, BlackRose," I heard Chimney say from behind me.

I turned and used a motion command to bow. Nova appeared a moment later.

"Hey, hey, were you here when the server went down yesterday?" Chimney asked.

"So far CyberConnect hasn't given any explanation. People are speculating it might have been a virus," Nova said.

I could never tell them I was the cause, so instead I asked, "Were you online?"

"Yeah. *I* was, anyway. *He* was AFK in the bathroom," Nova pointed at Chimney.

"He was what?" I asked.

"Oh, I keep forgetting you're a newbie. AFK means 'away from keyboard.' "

"I missed out!" said Chimney. "Nova said there was some strange voice. I wanted to hear it too."

He clearly has no idea how dangerous it was!

"Be glad you missed it. That weird noise made my head hurt. It was pretty awful!" Nova said.

At least that's all it was to the other players who were online. I felt a mixture of guilt and relief.

"So you were all right?" I asked.

"Hmm?" Nova replied. "Yeah, I guess. I mean, there's nothing wrong with my character data or my computer."

"Then all's well that ends well," Chimney said.

"Yeah, except I'd just found a Gott Statue treasure, and the noise made me drop it. I think I'm going to go back and look for it. How about you, BlackRose? What are you up to?" Nova inquired.

"Uh, I've got something to do," I answered ambiguously.

"Too bad. Well, we're heading out then." Chimney waved cheerfully.

Nova looked as if he were about to speak, but he ended up holding back. Perhaps he suspected something.

I wondered if I could confide in Nova, then decided I shouldn't. Nova was a good guy, and very smart, but I didn't want to get him involved in this.

Kite appeared a moment later.

"Come on! Let's go!" I said cheerfully. "Let's see if we can figure out what happened!"

"That thing might still be there," Kite said ominously. "It's too dangerous!"

"Don't you think I know that? Do you really think I *want* to go back there? I just know we have to, and I don't want to go alone. So unless you're fine leaving things the way they are, let's quit arguing and get on with it."

Kite didn't reply.

"*Are* you fine leaving things the way they are?" I asked.

"No," Kite replied.

More silence.

"You aren't thinking of going there *alone* again, are you?" I asked.

Kite didn't answer. I knew the answer was *yes*.

"Are you nuts?! You can't do this alone. Even though we managed to defeat Skeith, it didn't bring . . ." I couldn't finish my thought. *Even though we managed to defeat Skeith, it didn't bring Fumikazu or Orca back.*

"We have no choice but to return, so let's go!" I continued. "Hurry and invite me."

I stared into Kite's CG eyes, wishing I could see the real person behind the avatar.

"Okay. Let's be sure," he said.

● ⬢ ●

Everything looked exactly as it had before. In other words, it looked like its name described—hopeless.

We walked through the broken landscape without a word, then headed for the deepest part of the dungeon.

"The bracelet's not shining," Kite pointed out.

Something was amiss. It wasn't just the bracelet; it felt like there was something different about this place now.

I carefully surveyed the surroundings. Then it hit me—there weren't any magic portals.

We entered the dungeon and quickly made our way down. Nothing impeded us.

"There are no enemies," Kite commented.

"Maybe this area is no longer functioning?" I suggested.

Kite continued forward in silence, which only made me feel more anxious, so I asked Kite, "You think that thing will be there?"

"Yeah, maybe."

"If it's there, do you think we can win?"

"Well . . ." Kite paused a moment. "No."

He said it so casually, it felt crushing. But he was right. We couldn't win against something so immense. Maybe part of why I trusted Kite was because he was so honest and blunt.

"Can I ask you something?"

He nodded. "What?"

"Aren't you afraid?"

"Me? I'm not afraid. You?"

"Yeah, a little," I answered.

"To be honest, I'm terrified," he confessed. "But I can't let that stop me now."

At least we both feel the same way. He was right. Until Fumikazu woke up, I couldn't run away. Kite's simple confession warmed my heart—I wasn't alone. Maybe like the tennis match, if I kept trying there would come a day when I was rewarded. I just had to stay strong.

I looked at Kite and wondered if I could tell him about my brother and how guilty I felt for choosing the words that ultimately put him in a coma. If I told him, maybe that would help shift some of the heavy weight he was carrying off his shoulders. Maybe he wouldn't keep trying to do everything by himself. But what would he think of me, a girl who caused her own brother to get hurt?

"Ah!" Kite suddenly yelled.

"What, what?!" I jumped back.

"Sorry! A data rift opened in the wall. It startled the hell out of me. I thought it was a Data Bug."

"Don't ever scare me like that again." I laughed nervously.

"It's not funny—don't you dare laugh at me!"

"Excuse me," I said. "But weren't you the one laughing at me when that goblin freaked me out at the church in Hidden, Forbidden, Holy Ground?"

"Well, yeah, but that was different."

"How so?" I asked.

"That was funny!"

"You mean it was funny because it happened to *me!*"

"I mean, come on. It was just a stupid goblin." He shrugged.

"At least it was a *creature.* You screamed like a little girl over a few strings of computer code."

"Okay, you got me . . . Why don't you go on and really laugh it up?" But then Kite turned to me, completely serious. "I want to ask you something," he said, carefully choosing his words.

"*Now* what?"

"I'm here to help Orca. But why are *you* here?"

Just what I'd been thinking about! I'd thought about telling him earlier, but never found the right moment. Now that I had the chance, the words escaped me.

Before I could answer, I heard footsteps behind us. I jumped behind Kite.

From around the corner marched a familiar tall knight in silver and blue armor. I took in those beautiful wings (whose defensive purpose was unfathomable to me, but I wasn't complaining). *Balmung! Why'd he show up just as I was about to tell Kite about my brother?*

"You again!" he yelled. "I come here to discover the cause of yesterday's meltdown and I find *you*. Explain!"

Why is he always yelling? I wondered.

"I already told you the other day," Kite replied flatly.

"You did?" I said. Then I turned to Balmung. "Well, if he did, then you already know why we're here. So what's the problem?"

Balmung looked at me. "I understand, but you need to face the facts. Whenever you two are involved, everything takes a turn for the worse. Am I wrong?"

Before we could answer, he turned and walked away. I watched as he disappeared into the darkness of the dungeon.

"Man, I hate him," I said after he left. But I was troubled. I couldn't stop looking after him. *Why did he come here? How did he know this was the place?*

"Maybe he's just got his own reason for what he's doing, and it's different from ours . . ." Kite muttered to himself.

But what other reason could there be?

Maybe Balmung knew what it was that Orca had been trying to investigate in the first place. Actually, that was the natural conclusion. Perhaps if our paths crossed again on better terms, we could compare what we'd discovered and start working together. But I could not imagine what could make him stalk off like that.

● ◆ ●

Kite and I returned to town. We had explored every inch of the dungeon except for the final room. Just as we'd reached the last doorway, a set of iron bars had slammed down; we couldn't get past them.

We were about to part ways when an NPC resembling a merchant (just like the one I'd seen before) approached Kite.

I had an uneasy feeling. NPCs didn't normally engage players; it was usually the other way around.

"Greetings! You were previously chosen for the Power-up Campaign," the merchant exclaimed. "We understand that you have had the misfortune of receiving an item that is incompatible with The World. Please accept this powerful item, the Book of Absolute, in exchange. Please take it with our compliments."

Kite shrugged and fished out another book, which he exchanged, and the merchant vanished into the crowd. I watched as he tried to look in the book but then put it in his inventory when it wouldn't open. "It doesn't do anything at all, same as that last book," he said. "I don't get it. BlackRose, you ever hear any mention of a Power-up Campaign on the BBS?"

I shook my head. "Nothing. We've been members about the same amount of time, right? I've been paying attention to the BBS and all of CC Corp's official notices— if they'd announced any campaign by that name recently, we should've heard about it."

It was very suspicious.

● ◆ ●

There is an area I heard about that I really want to explore. Would you like to come with me?
　—Natsume

Huh. I guess she's getting attached to me. Natsume's invitation e-mail arrived shortly after I bid Kite farewell. Deciding I might as well go along, I waited for her at the Delta server Chaos Gate.

"BlackRose!" Natsume rushed over.

"It's been awhile," I said.

"Yes, it has! I've been fighting and raising my level," Natsume continued.

"So, where did you want to go to?" I asked.

"Hideous, Someone's, Giant!"

"What's that?"

"There's an event monster there. Someone I know told me about it."

"Are they joining us?" I wondered.

"Yes!"

"Who is it?"

"Sanjuro." Natsume's gaze shifted behind me. "Sanjuro! Over here!"

Sanjuro was dressed as a samurai warrior. He also wore an eye patch. "Sorry. Am I late?" he asked.

"No, I just got here."

"Who's this girl?" He pointed at me.

"This is BlackRose. She'll be accompanying us today!"

He waved. "Nice to meet you. My name is Sanjuro Sunaarashi."

I bowed. "It's nice to meet you, too."

"So, you're a Heavy Blade as well. Yep, that's definitely the best way to go." He tapped his katana.

The three of us formed a party. We had a Twin Blade and two Heavy Blades. *Only, who will help us with health recovery?*

Looking at our character statuses, everyone had about the same skill set. It wasn't encouraging.

"Do you mind if I get ready first?" I asked.

I rushed to an apothecary shop. I sold off every last bit of unnecessary equipment I had acquired while adventuring solo, and then stocked up on recovery potions, including antidotes to counteract poison, restoratives that would end curses, resurrects for reviving dead characters, and anything else I could think of, hoping it would be enough.

When I returned, we warped to Hideous, Someone's, Giant. We emerged on the platform of an airship that glided above the clouds. Several such airships hovered around a massive, rotating giant that was suspended in midair.

The Next Stage

I recognized it instantly. Kite and I had seen it from below. At the time, I worried that we might have to fight it, but it now looked less like an enemy and more like part of the scenery.

"This is amazing. What a view!" said Natsume.

Sanjuro jumped from ship to ship, making his way toward the center of the fleet. Natsume and I followed after him. The giant turned out to be a human-shaped ship with its entrance in the "mouth." Since there weren't many magic portals to slow us down, we quickly proceeded through organ-shaped passageways and chambers to what must have been the core of the ship. It resembled a boiler room, and in the center stood a single portal.

"I wonder if the boss is inside?" Natsume mused.

"Probably." I used a strength potion.

"Shall we?" Sanjuro ran toward the magic portal.

Isn't it a bad idea to jump in without a plan?

"I'm going too!" said Natsume, who then jumped after him, her Spiral Edge blades at the ready.

But right before they plunged through the portal, a large purple dragon with eight wings on its back emerged from it, instantly striking Natsume and reducing her hit points to almost nothing. At first, I feared it might be a Data Bug, but it seemed like a regular computer-generated creature. Except, this "parasite dragon" had 9,999 hit points!

I prepared myself for a long, drawn-out battle, like Mistral did when we fought Skeith. I moved to the back so I could devote myself to recovery.

Sanjuro quickly attacked, but the creature's hit points dropped barely a fraction.

"All we can do is wear it down," I warned.

This wouldn't be easy. I moved forward to attack, but kept a close eye on everyone's health meter.

"BlackRose!" Sanjuro called. "You think we can finish it off?"

"We won't win unless we do."

"Right. Let's go frenzy against it!" he said as he launched into a series of attacks.

I used a talisman for a magical attack, but it didn't do a thing. I had no idea event monsters were this strong!

The fight continued for a long time, and just when it seemed like our recovery items would bottom out, Natsume shouted, "Everyone use an attack skill at once!"

We each called out a specialized skill:

"Gale of Swords!" cried Natsume.

"Ray rack!" shouted Sanjuro.

"Calamity!" I yelled.

The parasite dragon's health meter suddenly dropped.

"One more hit should do it," I yelled, striking the final blow. The dragon staggered and died.

"We won!" Sanjuro exclaimed proudly.

"Thank you so much for helping me," said Natsume.

I realized that this was what the game was truly about—teamwork and cooperation to overcome huge obstacles. I was beginning to understand the appeal; I'd quite enjoyed myself. And I had really needed the respite. This was a welcome distraction from my constant sense that there was something gnawing away at the foundation of The World.

◆ ⬡ ◆

Again today Fumikazu's medical equipment whirred unceasingly, quietly regulating everything. Apparently from time to time his heart rate would jump up, but I'd never been there to see it. A nurse had speculated to my mom that maybe he was running somewhere in a dream.

Whatever was happening to him, I hoped he wasn't in pain . . . As I sat at my brother's bedside, I told him about our progress . . . or lack thereof. I told him about the strange room and our encounters with Aura and Skeith.

"Fumikazu, what should I do?"

Until that morning, we were at a dead end. Aura had vanished, and when we'd returned to that final room to find a clue, bars had blocked our entry. We had no leads. Then, I'd gotten a suspicious email.

```
TO: BlackRose
FROM: anonymous
SUBJECT: offering information


I might have a hint on how to revive
those who have fallen into comas. If
you are interested, please come to
Theta: Soaring Sky, Bounded, Abyss.
I will be waiting.
```

I had never posted anything on the BBS, so no one had my address other than the people I'd already met. And

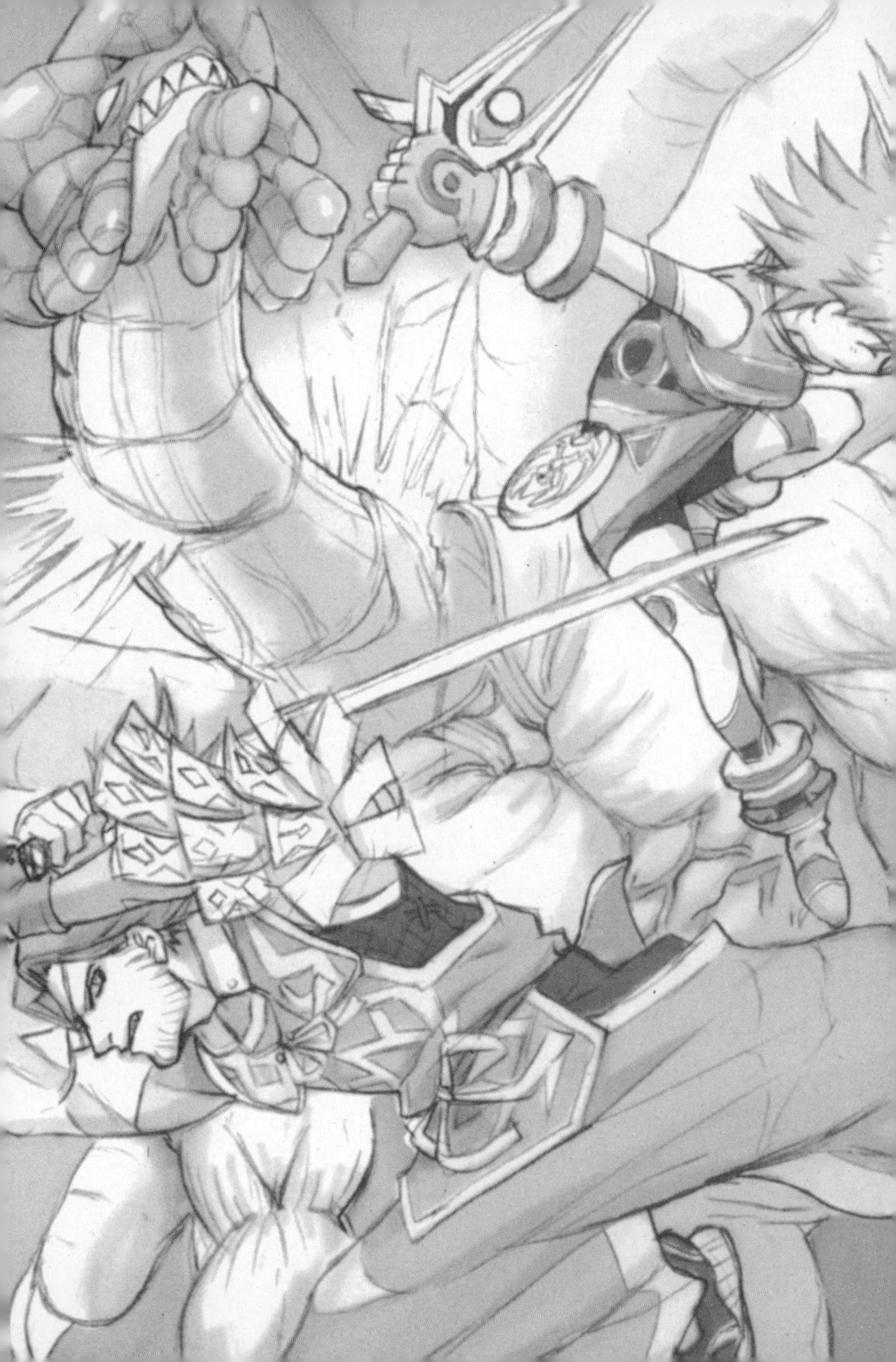

those who did know me in The World didn't know about Fumikazu. *So how does the sender know I'm interested in information about people in comas?*

Thinking about the strange email, I squeezed Fumikazu's hand. I could barely feel his body temperature.

"I'll find a way for you soon," I whispered in his ear. "I promise."

● ⬡ ●

Soaring Sky, Bounded, Abyss on Theta server was empty. There was no background, no landscape—nothing. It was an eternal wasteland of white empty space, just like the strange rooms we had visited before.

I tried contacting Kite, but since I couldn't reach him, I came alone. After walking around and calling out for a bit, I just stood and waited.

What the hell is this place? Is this really Soaring Sky, Bounded, Abyss, or have I been warped someplace else, like when Mia lured me into a different field?

I suddenly felt uncomfortably alone and vulnerable, and I wanted to return to town as soon as humanly possible.

Out of nowhere, Kite warped in front of me!

"Hey!" I called. "What are you doing here?"

Kite turned around, surprised.

"Did you get an e-mail too?" I asked.

"Yeah."

I felt uneasy. "Hold on a sec!" I wanted to find out if this was some kind of setup.

I opened the menu and selected "gate out." Rings of light coiled around me, but I didn't go anywhere. I tried again. Nothing.

"I can't gate out."

"I guess we're stuck here."

Suddenly, a high-pitched whine rang out from all around us; it was the same sound we'd heard when Skeith had appeared.

I nervously looked around, sword at the ready.

Bright lines shot through the air and converged on a single point, forming a cube. Stepping out of the cube was the merchant we'd seen before. Several more cubes appeared around him, and merchant duplicates of all different colors stepped out as well, all tilted at different orientations, floating above our heads.

"Welcome. I am Lios," announced the first avatar. "I am a system administrator of The World."

"You have ignored our warnings," said another.

"You have gone too far," said a third.

Warnings? What warnings? Then I remembered each of the times that I saw the merchant appear. Once it had spoken to Kite directly, trying to get his bracelet.

One of the avatars drifted lower and touched down in front of us.

"If the two of you hadn't interfered, the situation would not have deteriorated!"

He must have been referring to the fact that we'd knocked down the server when we took out Skeith.

"Us? What about *you?*" Kite lashed out. "Not only did you *not* do anything about the coma victims, but you also tried to cover it up!"

"Viruses, spread by hackers, caused the problem," Lios answered with contempt. "If you want to blame someone, blame them."

"How will blaming hackers bring back my friend?!"

I couldn't believe that the people in charge were taking this so lightly. *How can they be so irresponsible?*

"Fumikazu's still in the hospital." The tears I'd been fighting back spilled over my cheeks, blurring my view. "Bring him back to normal! Bring him back!" I shouted, my voice shaking. "Don't just sit there doing nothing."

My tears wouldn't stop.

"We are currently investigating the relationship between The World and those who fell comatose," Lios said dryly. "We are not taking this idly, I assure you. We're actively working on strong countermeasures."

"BlackRose . . ." Kite walked over to me, a look of compassion in his eyes.

"But there is one other thing," Lios continued, looking at Kite. "Preventing any further deterioration requires you to delete your character."

"Delete it? Why?" asked Kite, incredulous.

"Your character violates the software user's agreement. You have installed an illegal effect. You do know what I'm referring to."

Kite was silent. Lios must have been referring to the Data Drain.

"I will now delete you!" Lios announced. But before he could do anything, a woman's voice cried out.

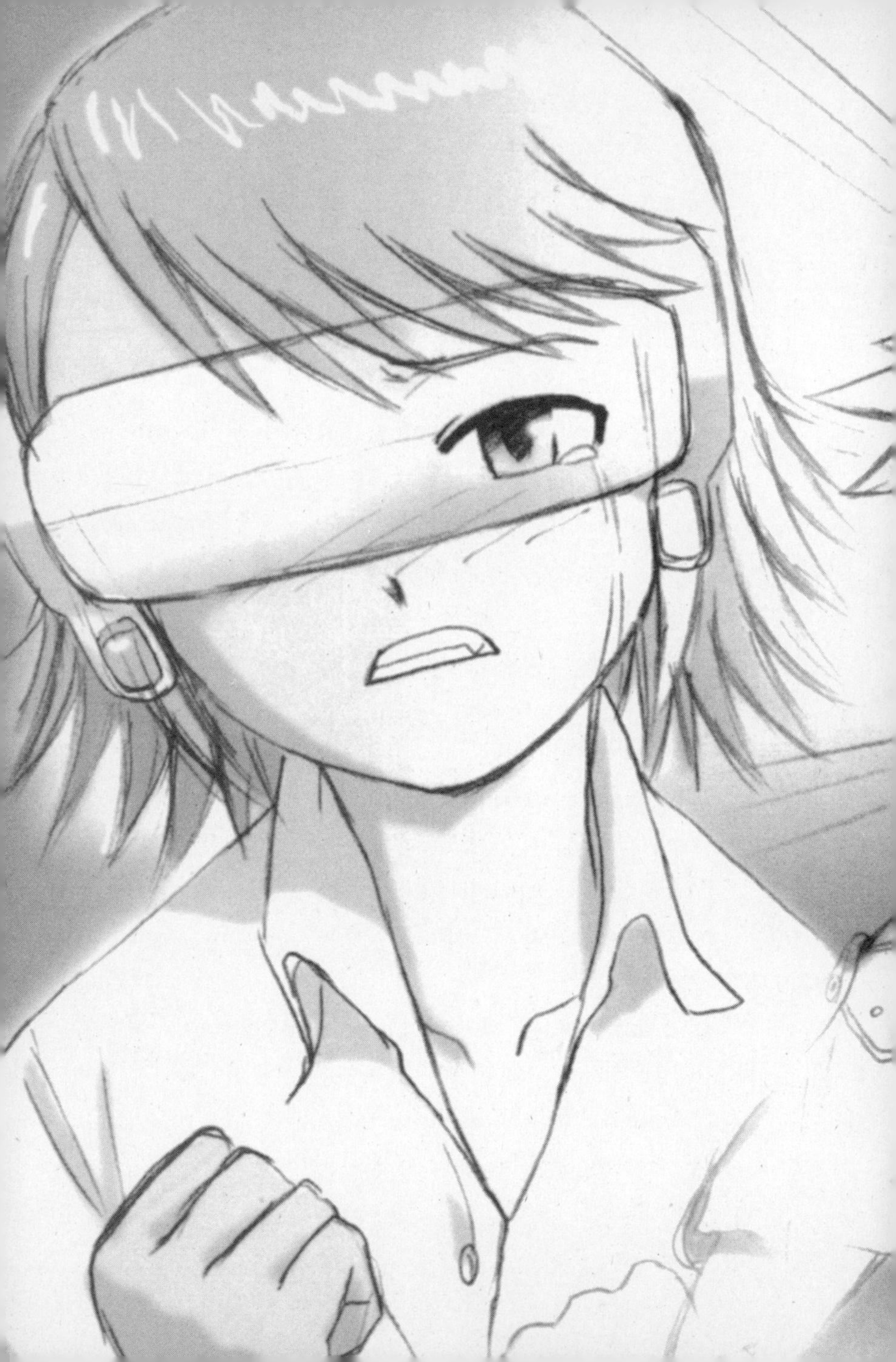

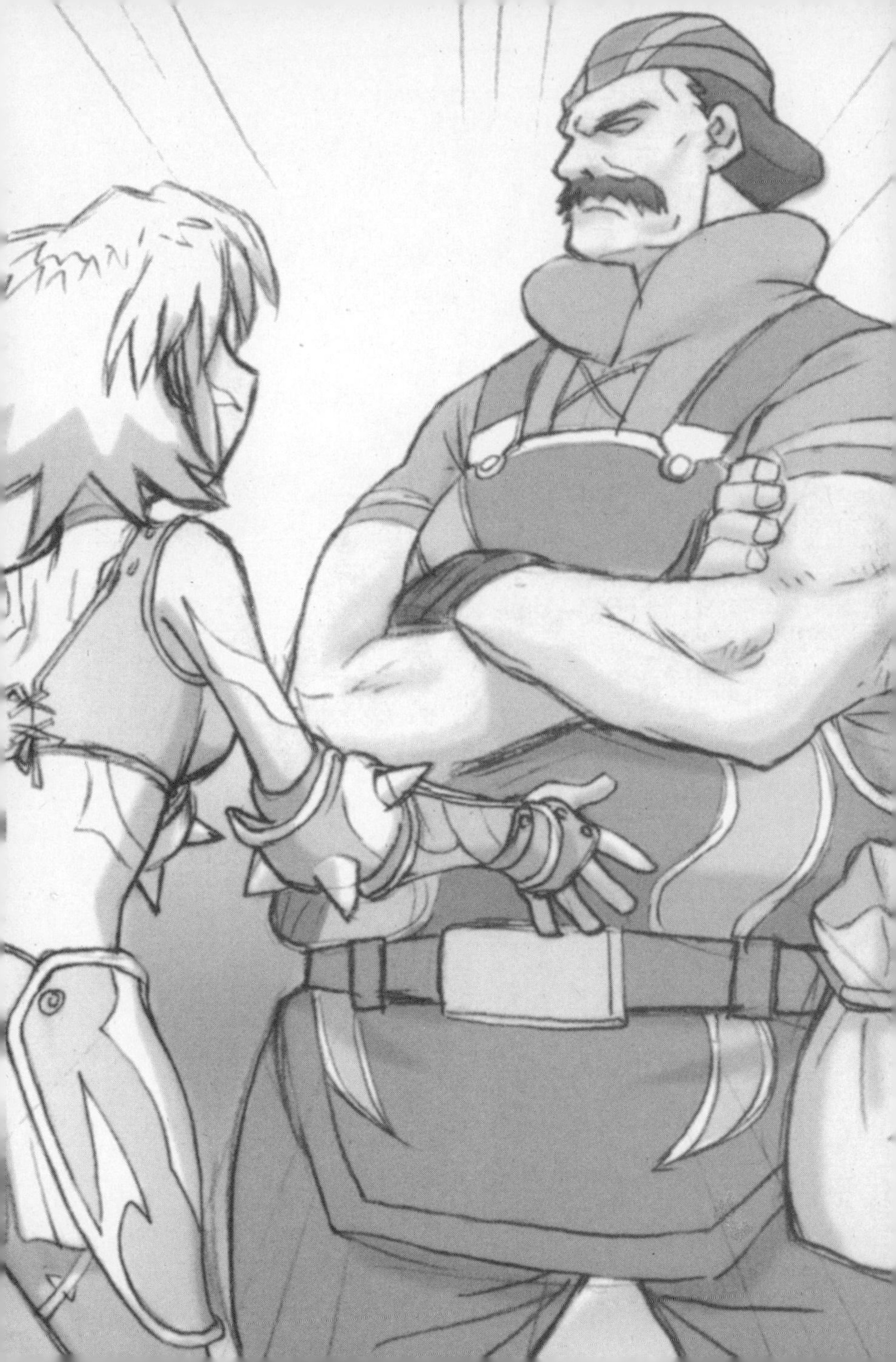

"Wait!"

The space next to Kite distorted, and a female avatar appeared.

"Helba!" Lios cried out.

"Lios, are you insane or just stupid?" Helba commented.

"W-what?" Lios sputtered. "How dare you?!"

"Don't act so indignant with me, especially when you're not in control."

"What do you mean, Helba?"

"I wonder what would happen right now if the boy performed a Data Drain on you," Helba said.

Lios gasped.

"No way! I wouldn't do that!" said Kite.

"I know. Because you're not stupid—unlike *some* people I know." She turned to Lios. "You don't even understand how it works, yet you're willing to delete it before finding anything out?"

She paused for a moment, then smirked. "Or do you even really possess the ability to delete it in the first place? Maybe you want it for yourself?"

Silence.

"The boy's character data has been so well protected that even you system administrators cannot rewrite it," Helba said, "even when you created a vaccine in the form of a rare item and tried to get him to use it. Don't you understand that what he's involved in could be the only hope we have of stopping the chaos? Deleting something just because you can't understand or control it is something only an ignoramus would do."

"Um . . ." Kite interrupted. "Can I say something?"

All eyes turned to Kite.

"I really don't care what happens to my character data."

Does he know what he's saying?! He'll be erased!

"Like I've said before," Kite continued, "I simply want to help my friend. And that's *all* I want to do. But I don't know how! Helba—and you, System Administrator—what do you think I should do?"

Helba sighed. "I'm sorry, my friend, but I don't know the answer to your question," she said softly, then laughed. "And I'm positive *this* ignoramus doesn't either. I can only give you a recommendation . . . I'm sure you've heard that the earliest version of The World was called The Fragment.

There's a rumor that The Fragment's design was inspired by the Emma Wielant poem 'Epitaph of Twilight.' Perhaps it would provide some insight."

Didn't the programmer who made The Fragment disappear? What is Helba asking us to do?

Lios snorted. "That's a dead end."

"Lios." Helba's voice was kind, as if she were patiently explaining to a child. "Lios is the codename assigned by the system to you as a system administrator. Were you even remotely aware that it refers to Apeiron, the King of Light mentioned in the 'Epitaph?' "

"It does?"

Helba laughed. "Deleting characters is not the only way to do your job. Instead of trying to hide everything in darkness, why don't you observe these two for a little while longer and see what they might shed light on?"

"I won't take orders from you!" Lios bellowed.

"Orders? I'm merely offering a suggestion. After all, if the problem escalates, won't you be held responsible? Right now, it's still isolated, but the net is a very large place. I can't imagine how bad it would be for you if it were to spread. But it's your decision."

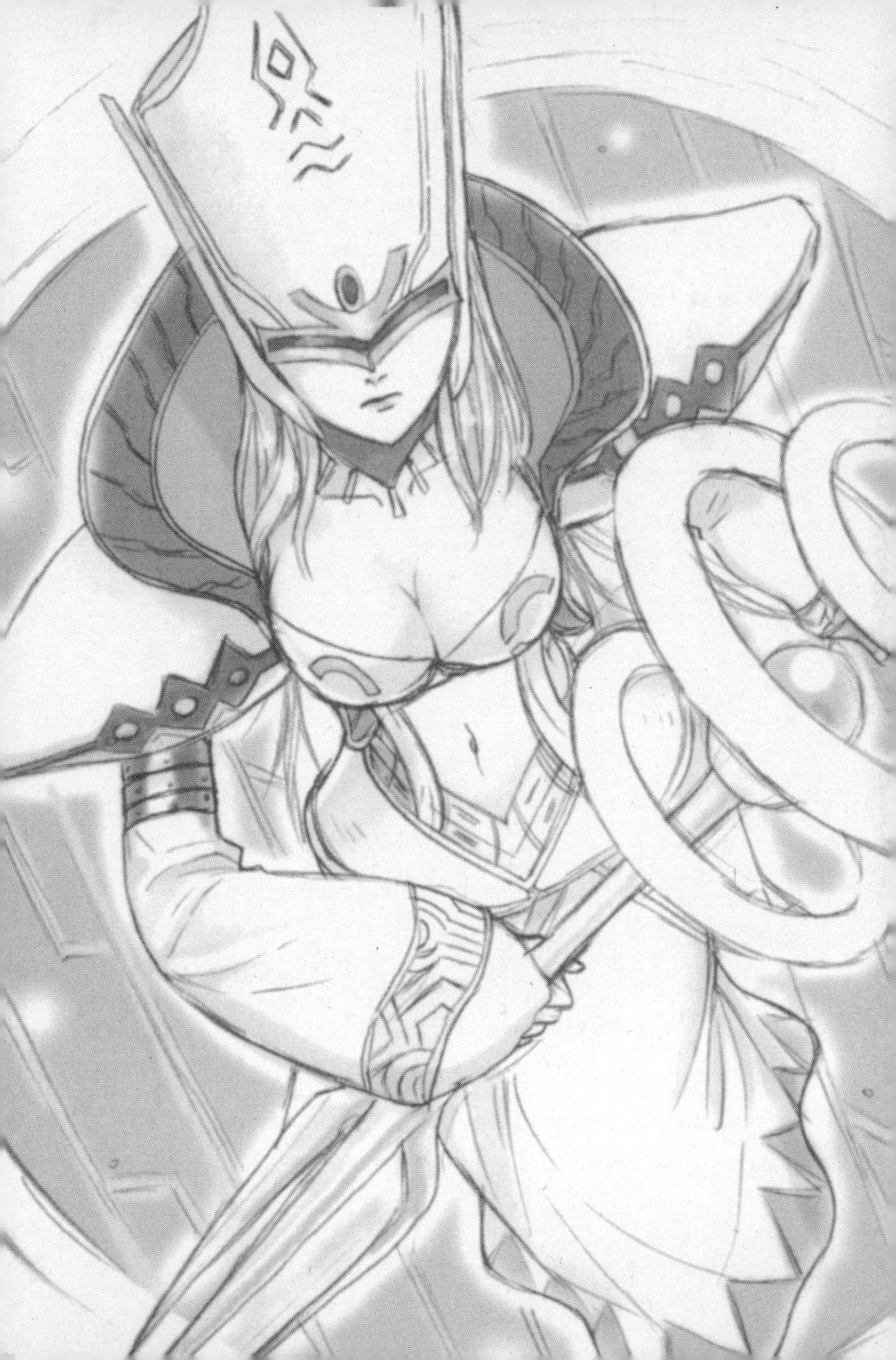

Lios sighed. "I need to think about this."

"Yes, try *thinking* for a change." Helba laughed again. "Who knows? You may find it suits you."

"You'll be hearing from me later," Lios snapped.

He and all the other merchants floating in the sky above us suddenly vanished.

"Well, I guess that wraps things up for now, my children," Helba said, smiling. "I'm sure we'll meet again."

Unlike her sudden arrival, Helba gated out the same way normal characters did.

Kite and I stood dumbfounded.

"Do you know what just happened?" Kite asked me.

"I was hoping *you* would be able to explain it to *me*," I replied.

At least we now had another clue. We had to search for the "Epitaph of Twilight." But why had Helba told us about it? *Who is she?*

In the silence that followed, Kite just looked at me. Suddenly I felt very awkward.

"Umm . . . about the thing earlier," I began. In the heat of the confrontation with Lios, I'd blurted out that someone close to me was in a coma. I thought, *Now's the time to explain it all to Kite!* But then . . . all my old doubts came tumbling back.

"No, forget it," I said, shaking my head. "Well, so long for today."

I've got to calm down . . . I can always tell him everything another time.

• ◆ •

The following day I received an e-mail from Lios:

```
I will consent to your actions
on one condition. From now on, you
will follow my directions. You can
continue your quest, but you will
work for me.
```

Suddenly, a whole new horizon unfolded to my mind's eye. I would no longer be playing The World as just a user. I would have access to volumes of information on the systems side. It would be easier to figure out what was going on now that we would no longer be in the dark.

All thanks to our meeting with Lios and Helba.

It wasn't long afterward that I realized how symbolic that meeting had been, after I finally read the "Epitaph of Twilight." I hated to admit it, but I felt a pang of worry. I wondered what it meant that the King of Light had tried to destroy us, but that we were saved by Helba, Queen of the Dark.

To be continued . . .

Postscript

The year since I entered this series' world has passed in a flash. It seems like only yesterday, I was discussing ideas for this series with my editors, and now I've just completed the first volume of my first long serial. I hope you enjoyed it. It sure has been a journey!

I played the games, so I was able to grasp the feel of The World, but the hidden depths of BlackRose's character were initially an enigma to me. Then, around the time the magazine serialization started, I went into the hospital with a high fever. While readers were checking out the prologue, I was vomiting blood from a stomach ulcer. For some unknown reason, my hair fell out, and I had to wear hats everywhere I went. And then just before I finished the volume, I had to go back in the hospital. I've caused a terrible amount of trouble for all those connected with this project, so I'd like to take a moment to apologize. I'm really very sorry.

I'd also like to thank a few people who helped me along the way, beginning with my teacher, who indoctrinated me when I needed it the most. Next, I'd like to thank President Matsyuama at CyberConnect2 for spending many long nights on the phone explaining the game to me when I didn't understand. To Tomcat and Waka at CyberConnect2, thanks for drawing the illustrations. To my editor, Mister T-mura, many thanks for taking care of me. To all my friends who supported me from the sidelines, I appreciate it. And to all the beloved people who took this book in hand—I thank all of you from the bottom of my heart.

I'm going to continue with volumes two and three, and I hope they'll be a fun read for all, whether you've played the games before or not. I'm still a bit wet behind the ears, but I hope you'll support my books for many years to come.

Miu Kawasaki

Art File

.hack // Another Birth

Akira has the same personality in real life as BlackRose does in the game. She acts tough, but on the inside she's just a regular girl.

In the game, the portrayals of the real people behind the controllers come across only through the words they speak and the decisions they make, so I worried about how to visualize her. I considered various approaches, but in the end, I decided not to vary her too much from the original BlackRose character design.

Akira's character design

Frustrated face

Dignified face

There's an odd key holder attached.

She's always rushing out the door.

When she has a lot of stuff to carry, she can fasten her bag on the front like this.

● The bicycle Akira rides to school

Sports bag with gym or tennis uniform inside

She may be enduring many hardships right now, but I'm sure someday she'll look this happy.

● Uniform creation (Akira)

DESIGNER'S COMMENTS!

Art File

The other things I had to focus on were Akira's school uniform and her tennis outfit. I didn't know whether I should choose a sailor-style outfit or a blazer, but ultimately, the blazer won, since everyone goes for the sailor thing.

Since I wasn't very familiar with the game of tennis or the kind of wardrobe it involves, I had to do a bunch of Internet research. I found some flowing skirt designs, but they felt too old. I also found a lot of plain uniforms that I thought would look better if I added some embellishments

Costume

● Uniform back (Akira)

KANAGAWA. ASAHI

ASAHI

It's more of a school symbol than a school pin.

The name of her school is on the back.

Rough sketch of how she dresses

She uses a typical racket.

She wears wristbands on both arms.

This is how the collars usually are, but Akira always turns her up.

She takes a big swig of a sports drink after exercising.

Akira attends Asahi Senior High, so I imagined a school pin based on the morning sun (asahi) and tried incorporating that into the uniform. Looking back on it now, it feels a bit gaudy.

Other than that, I thought of shoe designs, bicycle designs, and lots of other stuff that in the end never got drawn. Oh well . . .

Kazunori Ito

● Akira snapshot

She ties her laces before the match as she emotionally braces herself.

There sure are a lot of cool tennis shoes out there.

Akira prefers low-tops for less restricted movement.

The jersey is usually off.

She wears a jersey when it's cold. It's thin material.

Akira's underskirt is sporty and simple like this.

It's not too frilly, but looks like lace. It's too bad there wasn't much of an opportunity to draw this, but maybe next time.

The interval between pleats on the skirt is wide, and they don't go all the way up.

● Uniform design detail (Akira)